CONTENTS

Acknowledgments

Thank you to everyone who has made this book possible:

My parents, who instilled in me and fostered the creative spirit that makes me "me" and them "them."

My husband, Allan, for his endless support, encouragement, and understanding through all the times when my body was there but my mind was elsewhere.

My kids, Kristin and Jesse, for their unabashed optimism and humor even when they don't understand what Mom is up to.

The fabulous Michael Miller crew who stepped up to the challenge and made "it" happen.

Christine Osmers, the original can do personality.

The enthusiastic and imaginative designers who shared the vision and blessed me with a book full of wonderful projects: Marah Johnson, Susan I. Jones, Carol Kapuza, Ursula Page, and Marinda Stewart.

The professional and encouraging C&T family: Amy Marson, publisher, who has been supportive since the beginning; Jan Grigsby, whose vision and mentoring helped me complete this project; Diane Pedersen, whose creative sensitivity I trust completely; and Laurie Baker, who came to the rescue in the nick of time.

Kathy

INTRODUCTION

What is fabric paper? Fabric paper is the result of many conversations about the mounting excitement in the booming world of scrapbooking and paper crafting. During many trips to crafting stores for art supplies it was hard to miss the expanding aisles devoted to these art forms, not to mention the wide range of customers frequenting them. Back at the office, I made the remark, "If we could just package our fabric like paper we could be over in the aisles where the people are." One idea led to another and another and finally resulted in the question, "Why not stiffen the fabric to be like paper?" From that point on, with the enthusiastic input from the creative minds at Michael Miller Fabrics, we entered a whole new world. New product, new division (Michael Miller Memories), new market.

Once the product materialized (pun intended) and got into the hands of the talented designers involved in the making of this book, the ideas just kept coming. Everyone involved brought new techniques and tools for working with fabric paper to the book. And I'm sure there are more to come. You can get an idea of how many ways we found to use fabric paper in "How to Use Fabric Paper" on page 5. Currently, fabric paper is available in individual 12″ × 12″ sheets and packaged ensembles that include seven coordinating 12″ x12″ sheets and seven 5″ × 7″ sheets. Matching cotton fabric is also available for all of the fabric papers.

So, are you ready to try it? This book includes five party themes with lots of projects for carrying out each one. But don't limit the projects to a party; many of them can be incorporated into your home décor. And many of the projects from one theme will work for another if you substitute a different fabric paper. Have fun, be creative, and remember: If you can do it with fabric or paper, you can do it with fabric paper.

HOW TO USE
FABRIC PAPER

There are literally hundreds of ways to use

fabric paper. This list will show you some of

the techniques and tools that were used for

creating the projects in this book, as well as

some things we tried along the way.

Fold It!

Fabric paper creases very well. Use your thumbnail or a bone folder for sharper creases.

Heat It!

Use an embossing gun or an iron to heat the fabric and make it limp and malleable for shaping. The item will retain the shape you've formed when it has cooled.

Rip It!

Fabric paper will tear on grain. Use scissors to snip the edge of the fabric paper to get it started. If you prefer a more rustic look, you can pull threads along the edge to create a fringe.

Sew It!

Because it is essentially fabric behaving as paper, you can sew fabric paper by hand or machine, but you don't have to worry about it tearing or ripping like paper would. You can machine embroidery it as well, and because it has been stiffened, you don't need to use a stabilizer or backing.

Curl It!

That's right. You can make your own curling ribbon by cutting or tearing strips of fabric paper and then using the edge of a scissor blade to curl it.

Cut It!

Paper punches, die cutters, scissors, rotary cutters, craft knives, and paper trimmers were all tried and worked wonderfully. Basically, if it's a cutting tool, it will work.

Glue It!

Most designers and crafters have their own preferences when it comes to adhesives. Craft glue, fabric glue, spray adhesive, hot glue, glue dots, and glue sticks were just a few of the adhesives used throughout this book. Different glues give different results with different products so be sure to test your choice before using it in the selected project.

You're Invited

Print It!

Print directly on the fabric paper with your computer printer. Cut a 12″ × 12″ sheet to fit the standard paper size and feed it through your printer like you would a sheet of paper.

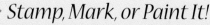

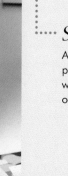

Stamp, Mark, or Paint It!

All stamp pads work well on fabric paper, as do marking pens and paints. There will be a slight variation in color when using the pearlized fabric papers due to the dyestuff on the surface.

IT'S GOOD TO BE 'TWEEN

You'll always think of her as your little girl, but in her eyes, your pre-teen baby is all grown up. That pretty pale pink bedroom with the ballerina motifs on the walls just isn't cutting it anymore and she wants a change. Redecorating can be a scary prospect at this age; her ideas don't even come close to what you think is appropriate. Never fear. She'll love this fun ensemble of room accents that rock with color and energy and you'll love the minimal effort and money it takes to make it happen. Invite a few of her friends over and make a party out of crafting the fun accent pieces. They'll have a blast and she'll end up with a space she's proud to have helped create. It's a win for everyone involved!

All projects designed by Marah Johnson.

INVITATION

Get the party started by covering a large manila tag with fabric paper. Print your sentiment on a coordinating piece of fabric paper and zigzag stitch across the top and bottom of the strip to secure it to the center of the tag. Add a row of zigzag stitching around the tag's outer edges. Use the small flower pattern on page 10 to cut 2 flowers from different fabric papers and layer them so the petals alternate. Cut 2 narrow strips of fabric paper for the "leaves" and fold them in half. Staple the strips to one corner of the tag and then glue the flowers in place over them. Glue a rhinestone to the center of the flower. Tie a strip of coordinating fabric through the tag hole and send your message on its way.

TIP Paper products such as the manila tag quickly take their toll on sewing machine needles. Use an old needle if you have one saved for craft projects such as this, and be sure to throw the needle away when you're finished making all your invitations.

ADDRESS BOOK

What 'tween girl doesn't make communicating with friends a priority? This fabric-paper covered metal address book is quick to make and so age appropriate that all the attendees will want one. Plan ahead so they can all embellish their own or have your special girl make one for everyone attending as a thank you gift. Start by spraying the front and back covers and wire binding with matte paint. After the paint has dried, cover the front and back with fabric paper. Decorate the front and back covers as desired. The book featured is embellished with strips of a coordinating fabric paper on the back and die-cut flower motifs and rub-on words on the front. If you don't have access to a die-cutter, the patterns for the large and small flowers are given on page 110.

TIP An address book with a heavy paper cover will work, too. Just spray the cover with a coat of gesso and let it dry before covering it with the fabric paper.

COMPOSITION BOOK

Dress up an ordinary composition book with fabric paper and ribbons and taking notes will be the coolest thing going! Spray the outside of the book with gesso to keep any pattern on the book from showing through. When it's dry, cover the book with 2 coordinating fabric paper prints. Hide the "seam" where the papers meet with a pretty embroidered ribbon. Place 4″-long lengths of grosgrain ribbon an equal distance apart on the ribbon and staple through the center of each length. Tie each ribbon in a knot over the staple.

TIP To keep the ribbon and trim from fraying, treat the ends with a seam sealant.

Paint Pail

Every possession in a kid's room is sacred but it doesn't hurt to have a storage container that clearly touts "my stuff" so there is no question about ownership. This container began as a new, unused paint pail. Lightly sand the outside surface of the pail and lid and wipe them clean with a dry cloth. This will help the paint adhere. Spray the pail and lid with flat white paint, and let it dry. Adhere fabric paper to the outside of the pail and the top of the lid. Cut out letters for the desired saying and apply them to a strip of embossed paper. Adhere the strip to the front of the pail. Tie lengths of a variety of ribbons to the handle and glue mini pom-pom trim under the top rim of the pail. Add a few die-cut flowers to the front (or use the patterns on page 110 to make your own) and you've got the best-dressed container in town!

TIP   Paint pails have handles; paint cans do not. Both can be found in a variety of sizes at most home improvement, hardware, paint, and container stores.

SCRAPBOOK PAGE

Don't let these precious years go by without capturing them on film. Whether she's into sports, drama, or animals, she'll give you lots of opportunities to show your creativity, and hers, in an album of scrapbook pages. Fabric paper makes a great background for whatever mood you're trying to set.

PARTY POPPER

Finish the party with a bang! This variation of the English noisemaker is a snap to make and sure to be a hit with the partygoers. Traditional "crackers" are wrapped with an easily torn paper, but we've used fabric that coordinates with the rest of the room décor. Don't worry; they'll still be able to get to the goodies inside. Center and tape the snap device inside an empty toilet paper tube. Cut a 6½" × 11" rectangle of fabric. Center the tube on the wrong side of one long edge of the fabric piece and wrap the fabric around the tube; tape the edges together at the tube center. Center and wrap a 4½" × 6½" rectangle of fabric paper around the tube; glue the ends together. Cut a 2¼" × 6½" rectangle from a different fabric paper.

If desired, apply a rub-on motif to the center of the strip. Center and wrap it around the tube; glue the ends together. Tie a length of ribbon around the excess fabric close to one end of the tube. Fill the tube with the desired candies, jokes, or novelty items through the open end. Tie another length of ribbon around the excess fabric at the open end of the tube. To create the noise, grab both ends of the snap device and pull sharply. Untie the ribbons to reveal the goodies.

MINI SUITCASE PURSE

This decorated miniature suitcase makes not only the cutest little purse, but it's also another idea for a unique storage container. Prime all of the outside surfaces with spray gesso, let it dry, and then paint the handle, sides, and lid lip with the acrylic paint colors of your choice. When the paint has dried, cover the bottom with fabric paper, letting several inches of the material wrap over onto the suitcase lid and back. From different coordinating fabric papers, cut pieces to fit the lid and back and adhere them to the suitcase. Hot glue mini pom-pom trim around the suitcase lip. Apply rub-on phrases to the sides of the suitcase. Tie ribbons to each side of the suitcase handle.

TIP This little suitcase can pull double duty as a gift box, too. Decorate it with the recipient's favorite colors and motifs and then fill it with an assortment of beauty products that will make her feel special.

COMPACT DISK CASE

You may not always agree with her choices in music, but there's no arguing that this decorated CD case is an artful addition to her room. Separate the lid from the bottom and then lightly sand the outside of both pieces. Spray the outside of each piece with flat white paint. Cover the top of the lid with fabric paper. Cut letters from embossed paper and glue them to the lid.

TIP   Looking for letter templates? Use the fonts available on your computer or look for one of the many books available that offer a variety of fonts. Enlarge or reduce the letters to the desired size.

BULLETIN BOARD

Keeping track of important "stuff" has never been easier or more attractive than with this colorful bulletin board. Spray a wood-framed corkboard with flat white paint and let it dry. Tear strips of fabric that are slightly wider than the wood frame. From these strips, tear 2 strips the length of the bulletin board for the sides and 2 strips the width of the bulletin board for the top and bottom. Staple the strips to the frame at the corners only. From one color of fabric paper, use the flower patterns on page 110 to cut 4 large and 8 small flowers. Cut 4 more small flowers from a different coordinating fabric paper.

Arrange the flowers in the corners of the bulletin board, layering the coordinating small flowers over the large flowers. Adhere the centers only with craft glue or a glue dot. Staple a 4½″ length of grosgrain ribbon to the center of each flower. Tie each ribbon in a knot over the staple. Use a heat gun to warm the flowers so they can be shaped. Curl some petals down over the frame and others up. Cut out fabric paper letters to spell "Notes." Center and adhere the letters to the upper portion of the bulletin board.

TIP A die cutter makes quick work of cutting out the flower and letter shapes. You can find die cutters for home use at many craft and scrapbook supply stores. Or, take your fabric paper to your local scrapbook supply store and have them cut out the shapes and letters for you, for a small fee.

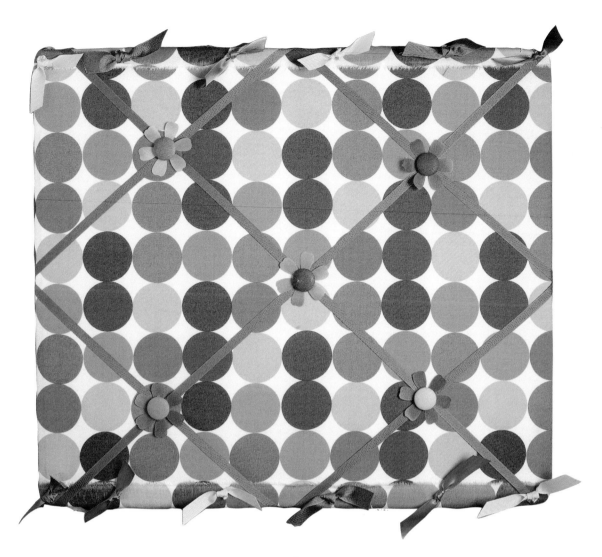

MEMORY BOARD

She can show off pictures, notes, and special mementos under the ribbons of this memory board and change them as often as she'd like without putting a hole in anything. Start by covering a premade memory board with white broadcloth and then a print fabric that matches the fabric paper you'll be using for the flowers. Be sure to pull the fabric taut over the board and work from side to side as you staple the fabrics in place. For added texture, tear 1½″ wide strips and staple them to the top and bottom edges of the board. Mark the center point of all 4 sides on the back of the board. Wrap a length of ⅜″-wide grosgrain ribbon from the top and bottom center points to the side center points to form a diamond shape, pulling the ribbons snug and stapling the ends to the center points on the back of the board. Wrap another length of ribbon diagonally across the board from corner to corner in each direction. Use the small flower pattern on page 110 to cut 5 flowers from fabric paper. Place a flower at each point where the ribbons cross. Staple through the flower, ribbon, and fabric and into the board. Cover five ⅞″-diameter half-ball button forms with the same print fabric you used to cover the board. Hot glue a button to each flower to cover the staple. Cut a total of twelve 6″ lengths from a variety of colors and widths of satin and grosgrain ribbon. Equally space 6 lengths across the top and bottom edges of the board and staple them in place. Tie each ribbon in a knot over the staple.

TIP If you don't already have a premade memory board to cover, use a wood-framed cork bulletin board instead. Cut a rectangle of high-loft batting the same size as the board, lay it on top of the board, and then cover it with the fabrics and proceed with the instructions above.

Mini Photo Album

The friends she makes during her growing-up years will always hold a special place in her heart. Keep them close at hand with this miniature photo album. Cover the sleeve of a mini matchbox with fabric paper and embellish it as desired. Cover the ends of the matchbox with fabric paper. Measure the longest side of the matchbox and cut a strip of cardstock that length, and 6¼″ long. Fold the strip into five 1¼″-wide sections. Unfold the strip and lay it flat. Glue a piece of fabric paper to each section on one side of the strip. Adhere pictures over each piece of fabric paper. Add any other desired embellishments. When the strip is dry, refold it. Apply glue to the wrong side of one of the end sections. Place the glued side on the bottom of the inside of the matchbox. Fold the strip into the box. Place the sleeve over the matchbox.

TIP Expand on this idea for a great teacher's gift. Take a digital photo of each child in the class and translate the above instructions to a regular-size matchbox. Place pictures on both sides of the folded strip to minimize the length of the strip needed, making sure to leave the section that will be glued to the bottom of the inside section blank.

Note Card

Corresponding by email or phone is much more common for the younger generation than using snail mail these days, but these cards are so fun and easy to make that you may find yourself buying more postage stamps for all the cards she'll be sending. Suggest she start by sending a handcrafted card to everyone who attended the party, thanking them for their help. To make a card, simply cut a rectangle of card stock the desired width and twice the desired height. Fold the rectangle in half. Cut a piece of embossed paper slightly smaller than the front measurement and adhere it to the front of the card. Cut letters for the desired sentiment from fabric paper and adhere them to the embossed paper. Embellish as desired.

TIP In a hurry? Instead of cutting your own cardstock, use premade blank cards. Eliminate drying time by putting it all together with double-stick tape or glue dots.

Asian
DINNER PARTY

Set the mood for an elegant dinner part with a selection of coordinating Asian-inspired fabric papers. Start by decorating your backyard to resemble a garden paradise, complete with hanging lanterns and glowing luminaries. Enhance the table setting with a bevy of beautiful projects that are easy to create and will keep your guests talking about them long after they've returned to their own homes. It's a party to be remembered from start to finish.

❀ INVITATIONS

Your guests will know their presence is requested
at a dinning experience they won't soon forget
when they receive one of these exquisite invitations.
What they don't need to know is how easy they
are to make.

Cut an 8″ × 8″ square from 2 different fabric
papers. Adhere the squares to each other, wrong
sides together. Fold in the corners so the points
meet in the center of the square. Finger-press along
the folds for a sharp edge. Use a ¼″ hole punch
to punch a hole ½″ from each point. Print the
invitation information on decorative paper. Trim
the paper to 6″ × 6″. Adhere the paper square to
the inside of the folded fabric paper square. Cut
two 9″ lengths of ribbon. Insert the lengths through
opposite holes of the fabric paper square and tie
each one in a bow.

FEATURING DELICACIES FROM THE ORIENT

SATURDAY, AUGUST 7
7:00 P.M.
5857 GLEN VIEW DRIVE

Designed by Ursula Page

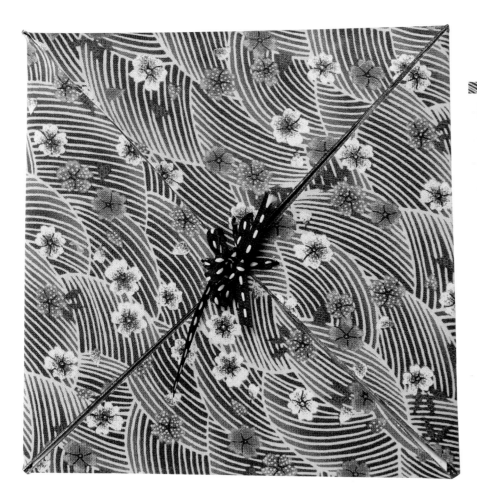

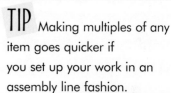

TIP Making multiples of any
item goes quicker if
you set up your work in an
assembly line fashion.

Designed by Ursula Page and Kathy Miller

This invitation starts with 2 pieces of fabric paper that are the length of the finished invitation and twice the width. One piece is for the outside of the invitation; the other piece is for the inside of the invitation. Fold the outside piece in half, wrong sides together. Cut out motifs from another piece of fabric paper and glue them to the front. For dimension, layer the motifs, separating the layers with foam dots. Sew a button or bead to the outside center front edge for the closure. Glue a loop of elastic cord to the inside back edge at the corresponding location. Glue the fabric piece you cut for the inside of the invitation to the outside piece, wrong sides together. Refold the piece.

Embellish the inside of the front cover with fabric paper cut-outs. Cut a piece of black poster board slightly smaller than the inner back cover. Cut out motifs from a piece of fabric paper and glue them to the poster board. Embellish the edges of the poster board with gold embossing powder. Glue the poster board to the inner back cover. Use your computer and printer to print the party information on vellum. Immediately after the sheet is printed, cover the wet ink with embossing powder and shake off the excess. Use the heat gun to heat the letters until the surface is raised and shiny. Cut the vellum slightly smaller than the poster board. Lay the vellum piece over the poster board. Punch 2 holes through the top of the vellum, poster board, and fabric paper. Secure the layers with a length of ribbon. Apply gold paint to the edges of the invitation.

Menu Card

Keep your guests informed of each dinner course with this scrumptious menu card. Small dinner parties may need only one menu card placed where all of the guests can see it. For larger parties, place several cards on the table or one at each place setting. Cover the front of a piece of poster board with fabric paper, leaving 2″ to 3″ of excess fabric paper extending above the top of the board. Print the dinner menu information on vellum. Immediately after the sheet is printed, cover the wet ink with clear embossing powder and shake off the excess. Use a heat gun to heat the letters until the surface is raised and shiny. Cut the vellum slightly smaller than the covered poster board and adhere it to the fabric paper with spray adhesive or vellum tape. Insert mini brads through the bottom corners of the vellum and into the poster board. Thread a charm onto a length of ribbon and wrap it around the top of the vellum, centering the charm on the front of the menu. Glue the ribbon ends to the back of the poster board. Cover the back of the poster board with a coordinating piece of fabric paper, leaving the same

Designed by Ursula Page

amount of fabric paper extending at the top of the card. Glue the excess fabric paper wrong sides together. Roll the excess fabric paper toward the front of the menu, stopping at the poster board. Run a bead of glue along the top of the poster board to hold the roll in place. Slide a bamboo stick into the back of the roll on each side of the menu.

TIP Personalize a menu card for each attendee and use it as an alternative to the place card.

PLACE CARD

Assign each guest a place at the table with these elegant place cards. Send the cards home with the guests as a memento of the party or remove the name rectangle and save the card for use at a future party. Cut a piece of poster board the width of the finished card and twice the length. Cover one side with fabric paper. Fold the covered poster board in half. From a coordinating fabric paper, cut a piece ½" smaller on each side than the front of the place card. Center and glue the rectangle to the front of the covered poster board. Use your computer and printer to print out each guest's name onto vellum. Immediately after the sheet is printed, cover the wet ink with clear embossing powder and shake off the excess. Use a heat gun to heat the printed names until the surface is raised and shiny.

Cut out each name so the vellum piece is ½" smaller on each side than the coordinating fabric paper piece. Adhere the name piece to the center of the fabric paper piece with spray adhesive or vellum tape. Wrap a length of narrow ribbon around the front of the card. Tie the ends together once, thread a charm onto one end of the ribbon, and then tie the ends again to form a knot. Position the knot and charm in the center of the top of the place card.

TIP Did you know that the best seat at a round table is the one facing the honored guest?

Designed by Ursula Page

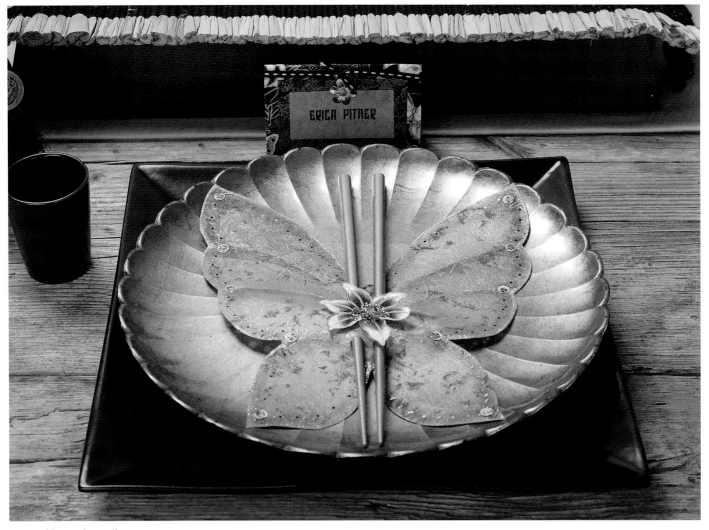

Designed by Kathy Miller

BUTTERFLY CHOPSTICK HOLDER

Even ordinary chopsticks will blossom into beautiful tools when presented in this lovely holder. Trace the largest butterfly shape on page 98 onto the wrong side of a piece of folded fabric paper. Lightly transfer the dashed inside lines on the pattern to the fabric paper shape. Cut out the shape and use a ¼″ hole punch to punch the holes where indicated on the pattern. Use a ¹⁄₁₆″ hole punch to punch evenly spaced holes ¼″ from the outside edges of the shape. Using a fine-tip applicator, apply clear-drying craft glue to the outer edges and pencil lines. Immediately sprinkle the wet glue with ultra-fine glitter and shake off the excess.

Cut a flower motif from another piece of fabric paper. Apply glue and then glitter to the flower tips and center. Glue seed beads to the center of the motif over the glitter. Attach a dimensional foam dot to the back of the flower. Center the flower motif in the center of the butterfly motif between the large holes. Insert the chopsticks through the large holes. For added depth, shade the outside edges of the butterfly with chalk or a stamp pad.

TIP For decorative chopsticks that will match your fabric paper, visit an Asian market or look for online mail-order sources.

Designed by Kathy Miller

SAKE CARAFE

Sake need not be served in a special container, but who could resist the clean lines of this simply embellished carafe? A narrow cord with tassels on each end, two decorative Chinese coins, and a small amount of fabric paper is all you need. Use the water lily pattern on page 98 to cut out one flower from fabric paper. Punch 2 holes in the center of the flower, ½″ apart. Tie a decorative Chinese coin to the end of the narrow cord above each tassel. Fold the cord in half. Working from the back of the flower to the front, insert the loop through one of the holes in the flower and back through the other hole. Wrap the loop around the carafe neck, and then insert the cord ends through the loop. Pull the cord ends to snug up the cord around the neck of the carafe.

TIP If the traditional rice wine isn't your cup of tea, a plain teapot would also benefit from this easy treatment.

WATER LILY
CHOCOLATE HOLDER

Designed by Kathy Miller

Serve up a sweet chocolate treat in this delectable holder. Use the patterns on page 98 to cut a base shape from one fabric paper for the lily pad and 3 water lily shapes from another fabric paper for the petals. Use the smallest butterfly pattern on page 98 to cut out a butterfly shape, placing the fold line of the pattern on the fold of a piece of fabric paper. Sponge a light coating of clear-drying craft glue onto the petal tips. Apply the glue to the right side of some tips, the wrong side of other tips, and the right and wrong side of other tips. While the glue is still wet, sprinkle it with ultra-fine glitter and shake off the excess.

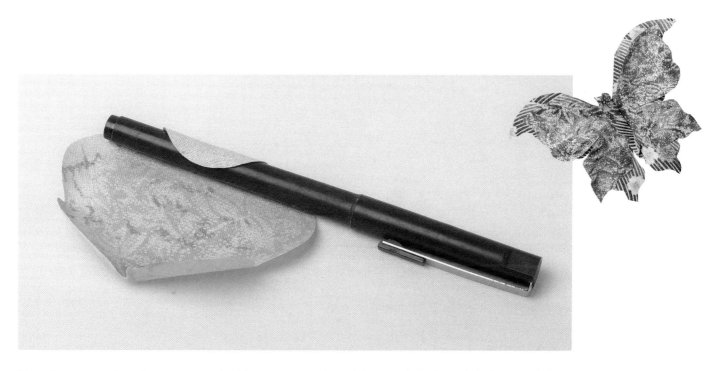

Use a heat gun or hair dryer to warm the fabric paper petals and the rounded edges of the base until they are limp and malleable. Roll each petal tip and rounded edge around a pen or pencil and hold it in place until it is slightly cooled. It will retain the curved shape.

With the right sides up, glue the 3 petals on top of each other, alternating the petal position on each layer to form the lily. Glue the butterfly shape to the wrong side of one petal. Position the lily on the lily pad. Place a piece of chocolate in the center of the lily.

TIP Hold the fabric paper pieces in place with a bamboo skewer while you heat them to keep from burning your fingers.

Designed by Kathy Miller

FAN

Talk of these fantastic decorations will be circulating through the party for hours. And to think that such excitement originated from an inexpensive paper fan. To decorate the fan, open it up and secure it in the open position with the attached clip. Spray both sides and the handle with flat black paint. When the paint has dried, embellish the front with gold leaves, and motifs cut from fabric paper. Add dimension by placing foam dots between layers of motifs. Embellish the motifs and fan folds with glitter glue.

TIP For added security, hot glue a portion of the handle together before you paint the fan to ensure that the fan remains in the open position.

TAGS

Add an extra flourish to your party with these dazzling tags. Use them to dress up a gift, tie around a napkin, or label food and drink on the table. You could even write a fortune on a piece of vellum the same size as the tag and attach it to the back of the tag to use in place of the traditional cookie. Cut the tag shape from fabric paper, using the pattern on page 99. Punch a hole where indicated. Refer to the tags in the photos for ideas to dress up your tag with dimensional fabric paper motifs, folded fabric paper fans, and touches of glitter glue and gold paint. Thread a length of dazzling ribbon or cord through the tag hole for the grand finale.

TIP These tags are great for practicing a new technique on a small scale.

Designed by Kathy Miller

MAGNETS

Designed by Ursula Page

There won't be a person in attendance who isn't drawn to these magnets. They make a lovely statement in or out of the container in any home or office, so be sure to make a set for each person or couple in attendance. Select magnets and clear glass pebbles that are approximately the same size. Lay a magnet on the right side of a piece of fabric over the desired motif and trace around it. Trace one circle for each magnet. Cut out the circles and glue them to one side of each magnet. Glue the flat side of a glass pebble over the fabric paper side of each magnet.

To make a container for the magnets, lay the bottom of the metal container on a piece of fabric paper and trace around it. Cut out the circle and glue it to the inside of the container bottom. Place the magnets inside the container. They will stick to the metal and stay in place.

TIP A craft punch that produces a shape no larger than the diameter of the magnet also can be used as the focal point of these magnets. Cut a circle from a plain fabric paper as described above for the background. Glue it to the magnet, and then glue the punched shape over the background circle before gluing the glass pebble in place.

CAMERA CASE

Make one of these cases for each couple and hand them out as the guests arrive. They'll find a disposable camera inside for taking pictures throughout the evening. Instruct them to take the cases home but leave the cameras with you as they depart, then develop the pictures and share them with everyone at the next party. Cut a piece of fabric paper 11¼″ long and 3″ wider than the longest side of the camera. With the wrong side facing up, fold down ½″ on the long side of the fabric rectangle and glue it in place. This will be the flap end. Fold up the opposite end 3½″. This will be the pouch end. Use a ¼″ hole punch to punch 4 evenly spaced holes in the doubled fabric paper on the sides of the pouch, positioning the first and last holes ½″ from the top and bottom of the pouch.

Cut four 9″ lengths of sheer ⅜″-wide ribbon. Place 2 ribbon lengths together. Tie one end in a double knot. Beginning at the top of the pouch, insert the ribbon through the first hole, pulling it through so the knot is flush with the hole. Weave the ribbons through the remaining holes. Tie the ends of the ribbons in a double knot close to the last hole. Trim the ends to the desired length. Repeat on the opposite side of the pouch. Place the camera inside the pouch. Fold the flap down and adhere a hook-and-loop square to the flap's wrong side and the corresponding position on the front of the pouch. Remove the camera. Embellish the outside of the case with a tasseled cord and decorative Chinese coin.

TIP Construct each camera case from a different fabric paper and use a variety of trims and ribbons to make each one unique.

Designed by Carol Kapuza

Designed by Ursula Page

TAKE-OUT BOX

Decorate your table with several of these classic icons of Asian cuisine, or fill them with fortune cookies or another after-dinner treat for your guests to enjoy. Remove the metal handle from a clean take-out box. Unfold the box and lay it flat. Cover the outside of the box with fabric paper. Use a craft knife to recut the slit in the box lid and make small slits in the box sides where the handle was inserted. Cut a ¾″ × 12″ strip from a coordinating fabric paper for the handle. Fold it in thirds, wrong sides together. Open up the strip, apply glue to the wrong side, and then refold the strip. When the glue is dry,

machine straight stitch through the center of the strip. With the craft knife, cut a small slit ¼″ from each end of the strip.

Insert a brad through each slit from the right side. Refold the box, using paper clips or binder clips to temporarily hold the sides in place. From the outside of the box, insert the handle brads through the slits in the sides of the box, going through all of the layers. Fold the brad ends out to hold the box together and the handle in place. Fold the lid flaps in to close the box. Add ribbons and other embellishments as desired.

BUTTERFLY STREAMERS

Hearts will be aflutter when you couple these streamers with the decorated paper lanterns on page 39. Options abound for creating the streamers, but in general all you need to do is cut out 2 or 3 butterfly shapes in graduated sizes for each complete butterfly on the streamer. Use an assortment of coordinating fabric papers and the butterfly half patterns on page 99. Place the fold line of each half pattern on the fold of a piece of fabric paper to cut a whole butterfly.

Layer the butterfly shapes together as they will be on the finished streamer, but do not glue together. Cut 1 or 2 pieces of novelty yarn and/or cord slightly longer than the desired finished length of the streamer. Choose several butterfly groups and lay them next to the place on the yarn where they will be attached so you can determine the spacing. The first and last butterflies should be positioned 6″ to 8″ from the ends of the yarn.

Slide the largest butterfly in each group under the yarn at the determined position. Place the next size butterfly over the yarn and glue it in place on the center of the butterflies, leaving the wings free. If there is another butterfly in the group, glue it over the previous butterfly in the same manner. For reversible butterflies, repeat the layering process on the opposite side of each butterfly. Apply glue and then ultra-fine glitter to the butterflies to decorate them with the desired design, referring to the photos for inspiration.

TIP Spacers placed on the yarn between the finished butterflies add another dimension to the streamers. For each spacer, use the patterns on page 98 to cut 2 circles of the same size from a piece of fabric paper. Glue the circles in place, wrong sides together, with the yarn sandwiched between them.

Designed by Kathy Miller

More butterfly ideas. Use your imagination!

If desired, create a dimensional body for some or all of the butterflies by rolling a rectangle of fabric paper around a pencil to create a tube. Glue the tube to the center of the butterfly.

Tie a decorative Chinese coin or a metal washer to each end of the yarn length. The coin/washer at the top can be used as a hanger; the bottom coin/washer weights the streamer and helps it hang straight.

PAPER LANTERNS

Simple yet elegant, purchased paper lanterns dress up for the festivities with a sprinkling of fabric paper butterflies and novelty yarns. If desired, glue a subtle novelty yarn to the vertical and/or horizontal lines of some or all of the lanterns. Follow the instructions for the streamers on page 37 to cut out the butterfly shapes and layer them together *without the novelty yarn between them*. Do not make the butterflies reversible. Use a small hole punch to punch holes along the edges of some of the butterflies so the light will shine through them. Embellish each butterfly as desired and then glue several to each lantern, attaching the butterflies at their centers only. If desired, add a butterfly streamer (instructions on page 37) to the bottom of some of the lanterns, eliminating the coin/washer at the top of the yarn length.

TIP   Decorate the lanterns that will be placed highest with simpler but larger butterflies so they make an impact from a distance.

Designed by Kathy Miller

DECORATED CANDLE

Melted wax acts as the natural "glue" to hold the fabric paper on this candle. Make several to illuminate the table as evening settles in. Cut a piece of fabric paper approximately one-third the height of the candle and long enough to wrap around the candle and overlap the ends. With a heat gun, warm the wax around the bottom of the candle just enough so the fabric paper sticks to the surface with the ends over-lapped. Let the wax dry and then blow the heat over the fabric paper again to make sure all of the fabric paper is secure. Cut out the desired motifs from another piece of fabric paper. Heat a spot on the candle that is not covered with fabric paper and immediately place the motif over the heated area to attach it to the candle. Repeat to attach the remaining motifs. Heat the entire outer surface of the candle with the heat gun. Sprinkle ultra-fine clear glitter onto the softened wax. Wrap a length of ribbon around the base of the candle twice, crisscrossing the ribbon at the back of the candle. Tie the ends together once at the front of the candle, add a small charm to one end of the ribbon, and then tie the ends together again to form a knot. Insert a small brad through the crossed ribbons and into the back of the candle.

Designed by Ursula Page

TIP CANDLE SAFETY

- Place your candle on a heat-resistant surface so it doesn't damage your furniture.

- Never leave a burning candle unattended or near something that may catch fire.

- Keep burning candles out of the reach of children and pets.

LUMINARIES

Traditionally placed around the exterior edges of walkways, these special luminaries will add soft light to any dark area in your yard. Make several from different fabric papers, following these general guidelines. For each luminary you will need a votive candle with a glass holder, and a round aluminum vent cover that is at least 2″ wider than the votive diameter. Spray the vent cover with 2 coats of flat black paint. Measure the lip of the vent cover.

Cut a strip of fabric paper the desired height and wide enough to go around the cover for the "chimney." If the perimeter of the vent measures more than the width of the paper, cut another strip slightly wider than the amount needed, to cover the gap. If you are using a fabric paper like the ones shown, which have a printed design that can be cut along to create a decorative edge, cut following the lines along the top edge of the chimney piece. Glue the chimney piece to the outer surface of the vent lip with the straight edge at the cover base. (If needed, cover the gap with the additional fabric paper strip and blend the top edge of the strip into the decorative edge.) Place the votive holder inside the luminary and adhere it to the center of the vent cover base. Place the votive inside the holder.

Designed by Kathy Miller

TIP OPTIONAL DESIGN DETAILS
- Use a small hole punch to randomly punch holes in the upper 2″ of the chimney for the light to shine through.

- Cut out motifs from another piece of fabric paper, embellish them as desired, and glue them to the outside of the luminary.

Harvest WEDDING

Every girl dreams of a special wedding and making it come true is easily achieved with these simple yet elegant fabric paper projects. Personalized just for you and your betrothed, the projects provide opportunity to express your individual style and share it with your guests. You'll enjoy every minute of the creative process and bask in the beauty around you as you celebrate one of the most important days of your life.

INVITATIONS

Start your journey down the path to forever after with one of these two creative invitation ideas. A trip to your local craft store will give you lots of ideas for items you can add to personalize them to your own taste.

An overlay of sheer fabric sets the mood for romance. Cover the outside of a folded piece of cardstock with fabric paper. Personalize the front of the invitation with a photo of the soon-to-be-married couple and any other desired embellishments. Attach the sheer overlay with decorative brads. Cover the inside of the card with a different color fabric paper. Use your computer and printer to print the invitation information on a piece of light colored fabric paper. Use decorative edge scissors to cut the printed fabric paper to the desired size and back it with a square of a different color fabric paper. Adhere it to the inside of the invitation.

Designed by Kathy Miller

Please join us
to celebrate
the marriage of

Tanya and Richard

Reception to be held
at the Castlerock Gardens,
Sonoma, California
at 3:00 p.m.
May 15, 2006

TIP Think ahead. Before you finalize the invitation size and design, go shopping and make sure a ready-made envelope is available for it.

Embossed initials create a simple statement for this invitation. Start by creating the initials on your computer. Use the mirror command to reverse the initials.

Print the letters on the wrong side of a piece of fabric paper. Cut out the letters. Cover the right side of the letters with VersaMark ink and then ultra, thick clear embossing enamel. Use a heat gun to heat the letters until the embossing enamel is melted and the letters are raised and shiny. Set the initials aside.

For the inside and outside covers, cut 2 rectangles from the same fabric paper the length of the finished invitation and twice the width. Cut a rectangle that is ½" less than the length and width of the cover pieces from a different fabric paper for the inside page. Fold the outside cover piece in half, wrong sides together. Glue the initials to the front, placing the first initial at least ½" from the folded edge. Fold the inside cover piece in half, right sides together.

Using the computer, print out the wedding invitation information on vellum. Immediately after the sheet is printed, cover the wet ink with clear embossing powder and shake off the excess. Use a heat gun to heat the printed names until the surface is raised and shiny. Trim the vellum so the invitation is approximately ¼" smaller on all sides than the folded inside cover piece. Open up the inside cover piece and adhere the

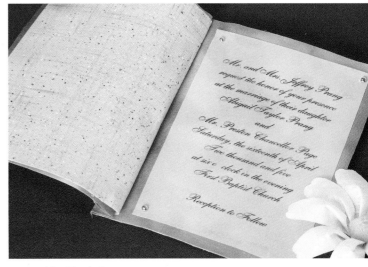

Designed by Ursula Page

vellum piece to the right-hand side with spray adhesive or vellum tape. Place the left edge of the invitation approximately 1" from the fold so it will not be caught in the "spine" when it is glued together. Insert a mini brad through each corner of the vellum and into the fabric paper. Spread out the brad legs on the back of the fabric paper. Glue the inside cover to the outside cover as shown in the photo, wrong sides together. Fold the page piece in half, wrong sides together. Use your computer to print out a sheet of vellum with a special sentiment or verse on it and emboss the letters as you did the initials on the front of the invitation.

Trim the vellum approximately ¼" smaller on all sides than the folded page piece. With the folded edge on the right-hand side, use spray adhesive or vellum tape to adhere the vellum piece to the top layer of the fabric paper page. Insert brads in the vellum corners as before, going through the top layer only. Apply glue to the wrong side of the page piece and refold the piece to adhere the layers together. Apply a ½" wide strip of glue the length of the page along the front and back of the left-hand edge of the page. Insert the page into the fold of the covers. Press in place to create the spine. Tie a length of cord or ribbon along the spine on the front of the invitation.

FABRIC PAPER FLOWERS

Designed by Marinda Stewart

No wedding would be complete without lots of beautiful flowers. As lovely as the real thing, these fabric paper varieties will stay fresh looking for many anniversaries to come. Mix and match the different flowers to dress up every aspect of the wedding, from the bride's bouquet to the cake. The flower petal and calyx patterns are on pages 99 and 100.

Preparing the Stem and Calyx

Cut out the calyx (pattern page 99) for the selected flower from loden fabric paper.

Overlap and glue the calyx ends at the pattern dashed lines to form a cone. Pierce the center with an awl.

Use needlenose pliers to bend one end of a length of 18-guage stem wire into a loop.

Insert the straight end of the wire through the hole in the calyx. Snug the calyx up to the loop and secure with hot glue.

Daisy

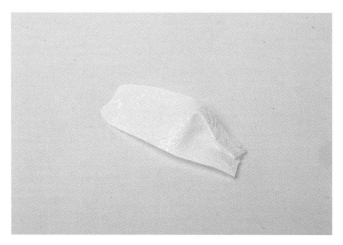

Trace 9 daisy petals (page 99) onto the wrong side of white fabric paper and cut them out. Pleat the lower edge of each petal where indicated. Secure the pleats with hot glue.

Cut out the calyx with pinking shears and prepare it as instructed in "Preparing the Stem and Calyx" (page 47). Glue it to the stem. Glue the petals inside the calyx.

Glue a ⅝"-diameter yellow pom-pom to the center of the flower.

Poppy

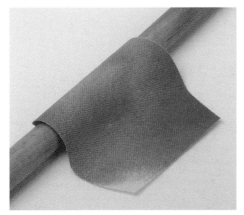

Trace 6 poppy petals (pattern on page 99) onto the wrong side of red, orange, or coral fabric paper and cut them out. Warm the tip of each petal with a heat gun. Place a ½″-diameter wood dowel on the wrong side of each petal and wrap the warmed tip over it.

Pleat the lower edge of each petal where indicated. Secure the pleats with hot glue.

Cut out the poppy calyx and prepare it as instructed in "Preparing the Stem and Calyx" (page 47). Glue it to the stem. Glue the petals to the flower center.

Cut a 1½″ × 12″ strip from black fabric. Fold the fabric in half lengthwise, wrong sides together. Clip the raw edges every ⅛″ along the length of the strip to create a fringe. Roll the fringe strip around the dowel, gluing around the fold as the strip is wrapped.

Remove the fringed unit from the dowel and glue it to the center of the poppy. Glue a ⅝″-diameter black pom-pom to the center of the fringed unit.

Sunflower

Trace 17 sunflower petals (pattern on page 99) onto the wrong side of yellow, honey, or flame fabric paper and cut them out. Pleat the lower edge of each petal where indicated. Secure the pleats with hot glue.

Cut out the sunflower calyx (pattern on page 99). Before gluing the calyx into a cone, heat the tips with a heat gun and curl them downward. Refer to "Preparing the Stem and Calyx" (page 47). to finish preparing the calyx and stem. Glue the stem to the calyx.

NOTE Other options for the center include rolling just the cocoa fringed strip into a center unit, or rolling a cocoa and a coin fringed strip into a center unit.

Glue 10 petals to the inside top edge of the calyx. Glue the remaining 7 petals inside the first row of petals. Leave the center empty.

Cut a 2¼″ × 12″ strip from cocoa fabric paper, a 2¼″ × 6″ strip from coin fabric paper, and a 2¼″ × 6″ strip from star-fruit fabric paper. Fold each strip in half lengthwise, wrong sides together. With pinking shears, trim the raw edges and then clip every ⅛″ along the length of each strip to within ¼″ of the fold. Roll the star fruit strip around itself, securing the folded edge with glue. Wrap the coin strip and then the cocoa strip around the light green strip, securing the folded edges with glue.

Glue the fringed unit to the center of the sunflower.

Iris

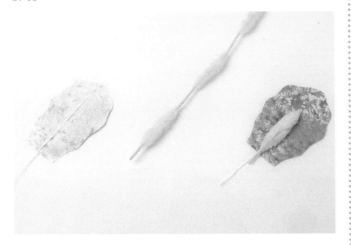

Cut out 3 iris petals (pattern page 99) from blossom fabric paper and 3 from plum fabric paper. Cut 32-guage white covered wire into six 4″ lengths. Center and glue a length of wire to the wrong side of each petal, extending 1½″ of wire past the petal's straight edge.

Cut the thin piece off one end of a thick-and-thin yellow chenille stem. Make another cut at the top of the next thick portion. Repeat to cut a total of 3 thick-and-thin pieces.

Glue a chenille piece to the center right side of blossom petal, with the thin portion extended beyond the end of the petal's straight edge.

Cut stem wire to the desired length. Cluster 3 plum petals together at the top of the stem with the covered wires to the inside. Gather each petal at the base and attach the petals to the stem wire using floral tape.

Place one blossom petal, right side up, between each plum petal. Attach them in the same manner with floral tape. Fold the blossom petals down, exposing the chenille stamens.

NOTE Irises can be made in two colors or a single color. The most common iris colors found in gardens are yellow and purple, but they are available in many beautiful colors.

Bachelor's Button and Carnation

From mermaid or celestial fabric paper, cut two $1\frac{1}{2}'' \times 12''$ strips and one $2'' \times 12''$ strip. Fold each strip in half lengthwise, wrong sides together. With pinking shears, trim the raw edges of each strip. With regular scissors, make vertical cuts every $\frac{1}{8}''$ along the length of each strip. Cut to within $\frac{1}{4}''$ of the fold.

Glue a group of purchased black stamens to one end of one $1\frac{1}{2}'' \times 12''$ strip. The stamen heads should be barely above the long pinked edge. Roll the fringed strip around the stamens, gluing along the fold edge as the strip is wrapped. Wrap and glue the remaining $1\frac{1}{2}'' \times 12''$ strip around the previous strip in the same manner, gradually staggering the folded edge upward to create a cone shape of petals. Add the $2'' \times 12''$ strip in the same manner. Trim off the excess stamen wire.

Cut out the bachelor's button calyx (patterns on page 100) and prepare it as instructed in "Preparing the Stem and Calyx." Glue it to the stem. Place the petal unit from the
previous step in the center of the calyx. Cup the calyx around the base of the petal unit and glue it in place. Heat the top of the flower with a heat gun and gently spread out the petals.

Carnation

Using the fabric paper color of your choice, make the carnation the same as the bachelor's button, but omit the stamens from the petal unit.

Tulip

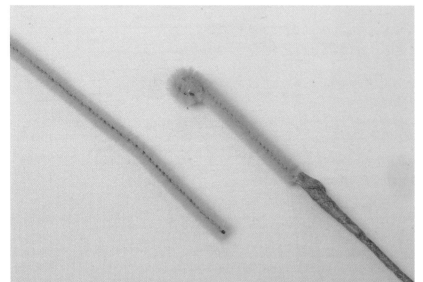

Cut a 3″ length from a yellow chenille stem. With needlenose pliers, twist one end into a tight circle to make the tulip stamen. Cut stem wire to the desired length and attach the stamen to the top of the wire with floral tape.

Cut out 6 tulip petals (pattern page 100) from shell fabric paper or the fabric paper color of your choice. Evenly space and gather 3 petals around the base of the stamen. Wrap 26-gauge wire around the base of the petals to secure them and then wrap floral tape over the wire to hide it.

Add the remaining petals in the same manner, staggering the petals between the already attached petals.

Rose and Rosebud

Select fabric papers in a dark and light shade of the same color. For the sample, we used shell (dark) and pink (light). Cut 8 small rose petals and 3 large rose petals from the dark color fabric paper (patterns on page 99).

Cut out the rose calyx. Heat the tips with a heat gun and curl them downward. Wrap the calyx around the base of the rose, overlapping the ends, and glue it in place.

For the bud, cut stem wire to the desired length. Tightly wrap one of the remaining dark petals around one end of the wire and secure it with floral tape. Add the remaining 3 petals to the stem as you did for the small petals on the larger rose.

Tips for *Making* Fabric Paper Flowers

- Use a plastic foam block or the equivalent to hold the stem while the flower is being assembled.

- A heat gun is a valuable tool. When fabric paper is heated, it can be shaped and molded. It will hold the shape when cool. The heat gun can also be used to "erase" shaped or molded mistakes and allows the petal to be used again.

- Keep a bowl of ice water next to your work area to dip your fingers into if hot glue gets on them.

- Use hot glue sparingly to hold the petal pleats.

- When the instructions call for shaping the individual petals, do all of the shaping first before pleating and assembling the flowers.

- Use tweezers to hold the petals/calyx when using the heat gun, to prevent your fingers from getting burned.

- When doing multiples of one kind of flower, prepare all the components and create an assembly line. Do each individual step on every flower and then move to the next step.

- These flowers were assembled with hot glue, but other quick-grab glues can also be used. Drying times will vary with each glue.

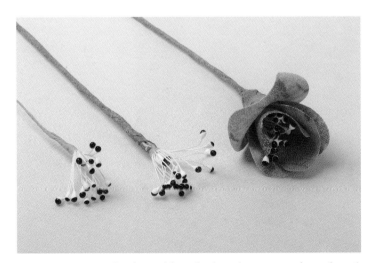 

Cut stem wire to the desired length. Attach a group of purchased stamens to the top of the wire with floral tape.

Adding 1 petal at a time, wrap 4 small petals around the base of the stamen, staggering the placement of the petals and attaching each with floral tape. Add 3 large dark petals and then all 9 large light petals in the same manner.

Cut 9 large rose petals from the light fabric paper. Warm the tip of each small petal with a heat gun. Lay a ¼″-diameter wood dowel on the right side of each petal and wrap the warmed tip over it. Set the petals aside to cool. Repeat with the large petals using a ½″-diameter dowel.

GUEST BOOK

You've got lots of important details to remember so don't depend on your memory on the day of the wedding to recall everyone who attended. Purchase a plain guest book and dress it up with fabric paper and ribbons instead. Cut 3 lengths of narrow ribbon approximately 2˝ longer than the book. With the ribbons extending above the book, glue one end of each ribbon to the top of the spine. Cover the spine with one fabric paper, cutting it the length of the spine and slightly wider. Crisscross lengths of sheer ribbon over each other the length of the spine and glue them in place on the ends.

Cover the remainder of the front and back covers with a different fabric paper, cutting the pieces longer and wider so they can overlap the spine fabric and ribbon edges and wrap around the book edges to create a finished look. Glue another piece of ribbon over the butted edges on the front and back of the book, wrapping the ends to the inside and gluing them in place.

Cut 2 pieces of fabric paper slightly smaller than the length and width of the book and adhere them to the inside of the front and back covers to hide the folded over edges. Drape the narrow ribbons over the spine. Attach a heart clip or charm to the end of one of the ribbons. Cover metal letters that spell out the word "guests" with acrylic paint. Lightly sand the paint when it is dry to scuff it up. Glue the letters to the front of the book.

TIP Refer to the invitation instructions on page 45 to make your own letters and coat them with ultra thick embossing enamel.

Designed by Ursula Page

PLACE CARD

Designed by Ursula Page

Small, round gourds are perfect for decorating the reception tables and displaying these colorful fabric paper place cards. Cut a piece of fabric paper the width of the finished place card and twice the length. Fold the piece in half, wrong sides together. Finger-press the fold and then open up the piece and straight stitch around the front of the card ⅛″ from the edges and fold mark. From the same fabric paper, cut out a piece that is ⅜″ smaller on all sides than the front of the stitched piece. Glue this piece to a different fabric paper. Cut ⅛″ from the edges of the top fabric paper piece so that a small amount of the different fabric paper is visible.

TIP Add just a touch of glitz to the place card by stitching around the edges with decorative thread. Go a step further by using a decorative stitch rather than a straight stitch.

Use your computer and printer to print each guest's name on vellum. Immediately after the printer is finished printing, cover the wet ink with clear embossing powder and shake off the excess. Use a heat gun to heat the letters until they are raised and shiny. Cut out each name piece so that it is ⅛″ smaller on all sides than the layered fabric paper piece. Adhere the name piece to the layered fabric paper piece with spray adhesive or vellum tape. Center and glue the name piece to the front of the place card.

Cut a 10″ length of heavy wire. (We used wire coat hangers.) Bend the wire in half. Apply glue to the wrong side of the back half of the place card. Lay the wire on the glue with the bent edge at the fold. Fold the top of the place card over the back and press it into place.

WATER LILY CHOCOLATE HOLDER

Chocolate is a symbol of love, so what better place to enjoy it than at a wedding? These sweet holders are the perfect accompaniment for serving the delicious confection. Follow the instructions for the Asian Dinner Party chocolate holder on page 30, but eliminate the glitter application. Rub a piece of chalk that is a slightly darker color than the lily pad fabric paper around the edges of the lily pad to add definition.

Designed by Kathy Miller

TIP Dreams that feature chocolate are a prediction of good health and contentment.

WISH TAGS

Let your guests share their best wishes for you, or you can share your wishes with the guests; these wish tags can work both ways. Set out blank tags for your guests to write a short sentiment and hang in a small tree for you to enjoy later, or write your own sentiments on the tags and let guests take one off the tree as they arrive at the reception. Use the patterns on page 99 to cut the tag base and motif from different fabric papers. Cut a rectangle of vellum that is smaller than the tag for each one. Layer the fabric paper tag with the vellum rectangle and motif. Use a ⅛" hole punch to punch a hole through the layers at the top of the tag. Fold a length of ribbon in half and insert the loop through the hole. Pull the ribbon ends through the loop. Knot the ends of the ribbon together to form a loop for hanging.

Designed by Kathy Miller

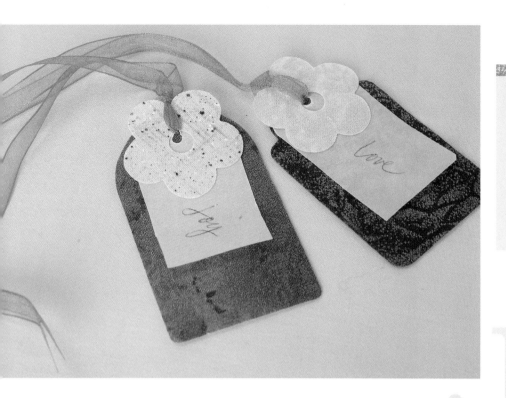

TIP Have someone take a picture of you and your soon-to-be spouse. Reduce it to a size slightly smaller than the fabric paper tag. Photocopy the picture onto vellum and use it in place of the blank vellum piece

JOY

COVERED MATCHBOXES

Inspire your guests to light their own romantic fires with these easy-to-make party favors. Just slip off the sleeve of a mini matchbox and cover it with fabric paper. Decorate the top with rub-on words, stickers, ribbons, charms, or any other love-inspired embellishment.

TIP Blank matchboxes typically are available without the matches so you can fill them with anything—verses, candy, or small wedding memorabilia.

Designed by Ursula Page

Designed by Ursula Page

FAVOR BOXES

Give larger party favors a home in one of these decorated pillow boxes. Carefully undo the pillow box at the glued seam. Cover the right side of the flattened box with fabric paper. Glue the box back together along the previously glued seam. Decorate the top with an embellishment that represents your special day.

TIP While the box is unglued, trace the shape on to paper to create your own pattern. Cut more boxes from poster board.

CAMERA BAG

You won't miss a moment of the celebration if you place several of these pretty bags on the reception tables. Inside, your guests will find a disposable camera so they can take candid shots throughout the evening. Develop the film after the reception and enjoy them for the rest of your life. Wrap a piece of decorative tissue paper around a disposable camera and insert it into a purchased sheer drawstring bag. Sprinkle several silk flower petals and sequins into the bag. Pull the drawstrings to close the bag. Use the pattern on page 99 to cut out a tag from fabric paper. Use your computer and printer to print out a special sentiment onto vellum. For our sample we printed "thank you for joining us to celebrate this special day."

> **TIP** For added interest, trim the bottom of the vellum overlay with decorative edge scissors.

Use the tag pattern to cut out the vellum pieces. Trim the sides and the bottom of the overlay so they are slightly smaller than the fabric paper tag. Place the overlay on the right side of the tag. Use a ¼″ hole punch to punch a hole in the top of the tag and overlay where indicated on the pattern. Cut a 20″ length of ribbon and fold it in half. Insert the loop through the tag and overlay holes. Pull the ribbon ends through the loop. Tie the ribbon in a bow. Place 2 small pearls or beads on a small gold safety pin. Insert the pin through the bow knot and attach it to the bag. Tie knots in the ribbon to finish.

Designed by Carol Kapuza

COMPACT DISK CASE

Designed by Ursula Page

Give the wedding attendants and helpers this special decorated case with a CD of their favorite artist. They'll think of your special day whenever they play it. Cover all the outer surfaces of a CD case with fabric paper, leaving the fabric paper along the top front edge unattached. Push a small decorative brad through the opening of a door knocker charm. Insert the brad ends through the unattached paper at the center front of the case. Spread the brad ends out and then adhere the fabric paper to the case. Apply a small amount of glue under the charm to permanently hold it in place. Apply letter stickers to a metal charm to spell out the desired sentiment. Wrap a length of ribbon around the front of the case 3 times and tie the ends together in a knot on the front of the case. Thread the metal charm onto one end of the ribbon and then tie the ribbon in a bow. If desired, glue the charm to the ribbon.

TIP Select a song that reminds you of each person who will receive a CD case. Burn a CD for each recipient with all of the selected songs on it. It's fun for the recipients to guess which song reminds you of them (and why), and it can be a great icebreaker if the attendants don't know each other.

Scrapbook Pages

Scrapbook pages are the perfect keepsake for remembering the special day and sharing it with others.

Designed by Kathy Miller

Bon Voyage!

What better excuse to throw a party than a bon voyage send off celebrating a friend's fabulous vacation trip? Whether if it's a trip across the sea or across the state, the travel gifts in this section are sure to come in handy and serve as reminders of friends back home.

INVITATIONS

Make the party invitation as special as the vacation destination. These three ideas can be adapted for anyone visiting any city, anywhere, simply by changing the fabric paper and trims.

Remove the sleeve from a mini matchbox. Cut the sleeve along one side between the strike plate and the top of the sleeve. Glue the bottom and the remaining long side of the sleeve to the matchbox. Cover the outside of the altered matchbox with fabric paper. Apply gold paint to the inside, and the folds and edges on the outside of the matchbox.

Glue 2 lengths of ribbon around the outside of the matchbox for the bands. Add a small decorative sticker to each ribbon on the lid lip to resemble the locks. Thread beads onto a length of thin wire and insert it into the lip for the handle.

With your computer and printer, print the invitation information onto decorative paper, leaving blank space at the top and bottom and making sure the writing margins will fit the size parameters of the matchbox. Cut the paper the width of the matchbox. Fold under the blank portion at the top and bottom and glue these to the inside of the matchbox lid and bottom. Add miniature travel stickers to the outside of the case, if desired. Wrap a length of ribbon around the suitcase and tie it in a bow under the handle to keep the suitcase closed.

Cover the front and back of a large manila tag with coordinating fabric papers. With your computer and printer, print the invitation information onto clear transparency film, making sure the writing fits the size of the tag. Cut the transparency to fit the tag and attach it to the front of the tag with a small, decorative brad. Glue trim to the back of the tag around the outside edges. Tie a length of sheer decorative ribbon in a bow and glue it to the back of the card to cover the brad legs.

TIP Make tiny travel stickers and luggage tags by resizing scanned or copied images. Cut out the small images and glue them in place.

• Use the pattern on page 110 to make a dimensional suitcase from two coordinating fabric papers, cutting the pieces as instructed on the pattern. Apply tiny travel stickers to the suitcase, along with a luggage tag on which you've written the traveler's name. Fold a piece of cardstock to the desired size and adhere a piece of fabric paper to the front for the background. Place the fabric paper suitcase onto the background fabric paper. Laminate the front of the card or cover it with clear self-adhesive vinyl.

With your computer and printer, print the party information onto a sheet of decorative paper and glue it to the inside of the card, making sure the writing margins will fit the size parameters of the invitation card. Wrap a ribbon around the inside of the card and tie it in a bow on the outside of the completed card.

Designed by Susan I. Jones

TRAVEL VALET

Keep all necessary travel documents handy with this multi-pocket valet. Personalized with selected fabric papers and coordinating beads, chains, or cords, this travel valet features places to carry a photo ID, passport, and boarding pass on the front side and a pen and a pocket for cash or a credit card on the back.

Start by cutting a backing piece 9″ x 5″ from fabric paper. From different fabric papers, cut a narrow rectangle for a pen pocket and another rectangle that is twice the measurement of the longest side of a credit card plus 1″ for the credit card pocket. Cut 4 pieces for the front pockets from different fabric papers, using clear vinyl for the lower ID pocket. The pockets should be the width of the backing and different lengths so they stagger.

Bind one short edge of the pocket with 1″-wide strips of fabric paper. Bind both short edges of the credit card pocket. The upper front piece will be bound later. Fold one bound edge of the credit card piece up, wrong sides together, to within 1″ of the opposite bound edge. Cut ½″ away from the sides of the "flap" end.

Place the wrong side of the pocket pen on the right side of the backing piece with the bottom edge and one side edge aligned. Stitch in place along the inside long edge only. Place the credit card pocket next to the pen pocket with the folded edge ½″ from the bottom and the sides aligned. Stitch along the inside edge only, keeping the flap free.

Designed by Susan I. Jones

TIP Make a fashion statement by using beads for the hanging cord, like the faux pearls we used, or dismantle an old necklace and restring the beads onto beading wire. Use crimp beads on each end of the beaded wire to ensure a sturdy holder. Decorative chain or cord also adds a distinctive finish.

Apply self-adhesive hook-and-loop dots to the pocket flap and the corresponding position on the pocket. Place the front pockets on the wrong side of the back piece so the pocket's bound edges are staggered and the vinyl piece is at the lower edge. Align the short edge of the unbound piece with the top of the back piece. Bind the edges of the valet with fabric paper strips, being careful not to catch the folded edge of the credit card pocket in the stitching. Set eyelets in the upper corners. Thread a split ring through each eyelet. Attach a strand of beads or cord to the split rings.

EYE MASK AND EARPLUG POUCH

Slip on this fabulous eye mask and settle back for an in-flight nap. An attached pouch holds a set of earplugs so you're guaranteed to arrive at your destination rested and refreshed. Quick and easy to sew, you'll want a set by your bed, too. Use the pattern on page 100 to cut one mask shape *each* from fabric paper, lightweight batting, and a coordinating cotton print fabric. Layer the batting between the fabric paper (front) and cotton print (backing) shapes. Stitch around the edges through all layers. Pink the edges close to the stitching. Tack the ends of a 15″ length of ¼″ elastic to the front of the mask. Stitch decorative trim to the right side of the front, covering the edges and elastic ends. Embellish the mask with rhinestones.

To make the case for your earplugs, fold a 3″ × 6″ rectangle of fabric paper to make a pouch with a flap. Stitch along the sides of the pouch. Attach hook-and-loop dots to the wrong side of the flap and the corresponding position on the pouch. Embellish the flap with rhinestones. Wrap the flap over the mask strap and secure it in place.

TIP Make an extra mask and earplug pouch set to keep near your bed at home.

Designed by Susan I. Jones

BAG SPOTTER AND ID WRAP

This bright handle wrap will help the travelers identify their luggage in a flash. A hidden pocket on the inside carries identification information in the event of misplaced luggage. Cut a piece of fabric paper 4″ × 12″. Lay the strip wrong side up. Fold the ends up 2¼″. Set the strip aside. Fold a 1″ × 6″ strip of fabric paper over one edge of a 4″ × 4″ square of clear vinyl. Stitch close to the raw edge of the strip. Cut off the excess fabric paper that extends beyond the vinyl. Cut two 1″ × 6″ strips of fabric paper. Fold ½″ of the short end of one strip over the bound edge of the vinyl piece, keeping the raw edges even. Repeat on the opposite edge with the remaining strip.

Designed by Susan I. Jones

TIP Save time when you're making several of these wraps from different fabric papers by using clear monofilament thread in the needle and bobbin.

With the sides aligned, position the vinyl piece on the folded fabric paper strip you set aside earlier. The bound edge should overlap the raw edge of one folded end by ½″. Tuck the unbound edge of the vinyl piece under the opposite end. Stitch around the vinyl piece, leaving the bound edge open to create a pocket. Stitch across the top of the fabric paper strips on each side of the bound edge, and then stitch around the outside edges of the entire piece.

Pink the edges close to the stitching. Apply self-adhesive hook-and-loop dots to the corners of the wrap nearest the pocket opening. Fold the opposite end up 1½″ and then fold the folded edge up to meet the bound edge of the pocket. Fold down the end with the hook-and-loop dots and apply the other halves of the hook-and-loop dots to the corresponding positions on the folded up piece.

SLIPPERS AND CASE

Designed by Susan I. Jones

Eliminate tiptoeing barefooted through airport security with these lightweight travel slippers. This footwear is a snap to stitch and won't add weight to carry-on baggage. Sew several pair, as they can be discarded after doing duty at the hotel or hostel. One package of Michael Miller fabric papers will yield a pair, a case, and a spare. Select one fabric paper for the sole bottom, one for the sole top, and one for the band. Follow the manufacturer's instructions to apply fusible vinyl to the right side of the sole bottom fabric paper. Using the desired size sole and band patterns on pages 100 and 101, cut out 2 sole bottoms from the vinyl-coated fabric paper, 2 sole tops from the sole top fabric paper, and 4 bands from the band fabric paper. Place 2 band pieces wrong sides together and stitch ¼″ from the long edges. Repeat with the remaining 2 band pieces. Pink the edges. Place the band pieces on the sole pieces where indicated on the pattern. Stitch ¼″ from the edges around the outside edge of the soles.

To make the case, cut a 2¼″-wide strip from a piece of fabric paper for the decorative band. Use a ¼″ hole punch to punch two holes ½″ apart in the center of the strip. Use the pattern on page 101 or a decorative punch to cut out 4 flower shapes from the remainder of the strip. Set aside the cutout shapes. Place the strip on the right side of one edge of a 12″ × 12″ square of coordinating fabric paper. Stitch along the long edges. Fold a ½″ pleat in the case 1″ above the decorative strip. Turn the fabric paper to the wrong side.

Fold up the edge opposite the decorative strip 3″. Fold the fabric paper back down ½″ to create a pleat.

Stitch along the sides of the case to secure the pleats and the ends of the decorative band. Punch a hole in the center of 2 of the cutout flower shapes. Thread a length of ribbon through the 2 holes in the decorative band. Tie a flower to the ends of the ribbon, and then tie the ribbon in a bow. Use a ¼″ hole punch to punch 2 holes ½″ apart in the center of each slipper band and the center of each of the remaining flower shapes. Place a flower shape on each band, thread a length of ribbon through the holes, and tie it in a bow.

TIP Stay safe by adding a piece of nonskid material to the bottom of the slippers. These are great because they pass airport security so easily!

Fabric Paper Party

MEMORIES BOX

Transform any sturdy box into a memory-filled memento of your trip. Simply cover the outer and inner surfaces of the box and lid with fabric paper. Attach a metal bookplate to the lid with small brads. Use your computer and printer to print a label on cardstock and insert it into the bookplate opening. Loosely tie a length of ribbon around the outside of the box so it can be easily taken on and off to view the contents.

TIP Give your next gift in a fabric paper-covered box and the recipient will be getting two gifts in one!

TAKE-ME-ALONG PHOTO FRAME

This unique photo frame tucks into its own pouch for traveling and is constructed to stand up for display. It makes a thoughtful gift for grandmas, your world traveler friends, or any "road warrior." Cover the front of three 3″ × 3″ squares of mat board with fabric paper; cover the back with a coordinating fabric paper. Cover three 2″ × 2″ slide mounts with the fabric paper you used for the back of the squares. Apply glue to the side and bottom edges of each slide mount. Center the slide mounts on the front of the mat board squares and press them in place. Glue the desired photos to lightweight cardstock. Attach a ribbon loop to the top of each photo. Insert the photos into the slide mounts through the top opening. Place the squares side by side on a flat surface with the picture side down, leaving ½″ between each square.

Cut a 28″ length of ¼″-wide double-faced satin ribbon. Run a line of glue across the center of the squares. Center the ribbon on the glued area so that an equal amount of ribbon extends beyond the edge of the first and last squares.

To store your frame for traveling, stack the frames on top of each other and tie the ribbon ends in a bow. Insert the frame into a pouch you have made from coordinating fabric. To stand the frames up for display, lay the photos flat so they are side by side. Tie the ribbon ends together so that the frames form a triangular shape. When you are ready for a change, use the ribbon loops to pull out the photos.

TIP You don't have to cut new ribbon loops each time you change the pictures. Just glue new photos over the old ones!

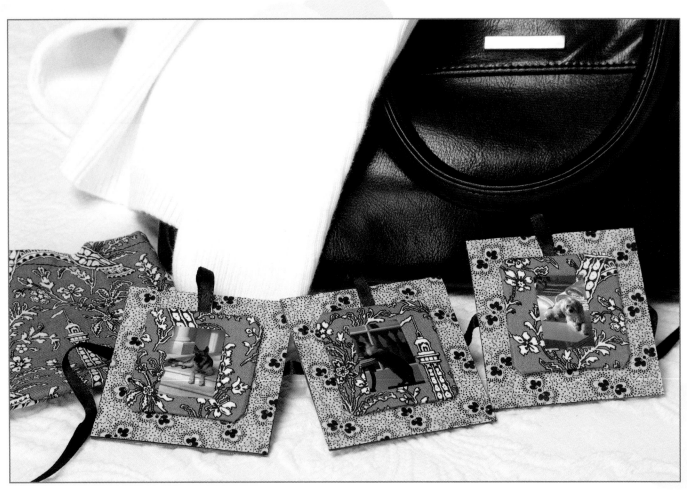

Designed by Susan I. Jones

PHOTO ALBUMS

Designed by Kathy Miller

sew close to the raw edge. Cut off the corners at one end and fray the edges for the flap. Bind the other end with a strip of fabric paper to enclose the raw edges. Place the book on the wrong side of the strip with the flap end extending approximately 4″ to the left of the spine. Cut two 10″ lengths of ribbon. Place one ribbon length, wrong side up, on the flap with the end at the spine center. Remove the book and stitch the ribbon end in place. Stitch the remaining ribbon length to the corresponding position on the right side of the cover on the opposite end of the cover strip. Tie the ribbon ends in a bow to close the book. Fold the flap over and attach a broach or decorative button to the point.

TIP Blank board books are available at craft and scrapbooking stores or through C&T Publishing, 1651 Challenge Drive, Concord, CA 94520; www.ctpub.com.

No trip is complete without scads of photos to share with friends and family when you get back home. Present them in either of these decorative albums and the viewers are sure to be talking about more than just your travels.

A ready-to-go blank 6″ × 6″ board book dressed up as a purse offers the perfect opportunity to creatively display your vacation memories. Glue a different fabric paper to the front cover and each page and then apply your photos. Add interest to some pages by framing the photos with a coordinating piece of fabric paper. Insert a piece of covered cord through the book spine to form a loop for the handle; glue it in place.

From the fabric paper for the outer cover, cut one 6″ × 11″ rectangle and one 6″ × 8″ rectangle. Overlap the short edges 1″ to make a piece 6″ × 18″;

Don't be caught showing off your pictures in a boring photo album when this one is so easy to create. Cut a piece of fabric paper the length of the spine and 2″ wider. Center the piece on the spine and glue it in place. From a coordinating fabric paper, cut 2 pieces that are 3″ longer than the album and 3″ wider than the measurement from the edge of the spine fabric to the edge of the cover. Cover the front and back covers with these pieces, butting the pieces up to the spine fabric and wrapping the excess to the inside to cover the edges.

Cut 2 pieces of fabric paper slightly smaller than the length and width of the album cover and adhere them to the inside of the front and back covers to hide the folded over edges. Wrap a length of ribbon around the front cover and tie it in a knot. Position the ribbon over the butted fabric papers and secure with glue. Cover the front of a slide mount with fabric paper and attach it to a piece of white cardstock. Apply a "friends" sticker to the cardstock in the opening. Glue the slide mount to the lower right front corner.

Designed by Ursula Page

LIL' COWPOKE
birthday party

Everything's ready down at the OK Corral so round up the gang for a rootin'
tootin' good time. The little guys and gals will enjoy getting into character to celebrate
your little cowpoke's birthday, and there's no shortage of fun to be had when these
fabric paper projects are on hand. Who knows? You may just have as much fun, if not
more, making the projects as they will playing with them.

INVITATIONS

Rustle up your computer and printer and a few supplies and you'll have these invitations ready for the pony express in no time flat.

Cut a piece of poster board to the desired size of the folded invitation. Cut 2 different pieces of fabric paper that are the length of the poster board and twice the width. Apply glue to the wrong side of the fabric paper for the outside of the invitation. Center the poster board on the glued piece, aligning the top and bottom edges with the fabric paper and having an equal amount of fabric paper on each side. Lay the remaining fabric paper piece over the poster board, right side up, and press it in place between the 2 pieces of fabric paper, wrong sides together. Apply fabric decoupage medium to the front and back of the invitation and let it dry. Fold the left and right edges toward each other along the sides of the poster board. Use a bone folder to crease the edges. Open the flaps back up and straight stitch round the flap ¼" from the edges.

Designed by Ursula Page

Using your computer and printer, print the invitation information onto cardstock, leaving blank space at the top of the piece for the fabric embellishment. Cut out the piece so it is slightly smaller than the poster board. Cut a fabric paper rectangle that is slightly smaller than the blank space above the wording. Adhere it to the card stock. Add a mini brad in each corner of the rectangle. Cut out a square motif from fabric paper. Zigzag stitch around the square. Adhere it on point to the center of the fabric paper rectangle. Center and adhere the cardstock piece over the poster board section of the invitation. Close the flaps. Tie a piece of hemp cord or twine around the invitation.

Designed by Susan I. Jones

Using your computer and printer, follow the tag pattern on page 102 to print the invitation wording onto plain white paper. Substitute the name, date, time, address, and phone information shown on the pattern with your own. Tear the paper along each side of the wording, always pulling the paper slowly toward you. Crumple the paper into a ball and then flatten it out. Use a makeup sponge to daub ochre ink across the wrinkled surface. Darken the outer edges with brown ink. When the ink is dry, use a permanent marker to write the recipient's name in the blank space under "Wanted." Use the tag pattern on page 102 to cut out 2 shapes from different fabric papers. Glue the shapes wrong sides together. When the glue is dry, stitch ¼″ from the outer edges; pink the edges, if desired.

Punch a small hole in the top of the invitation where indicated on the pattern. Set an eyelet in the hole. Refer to the pattern to fold the fabric paper invitation along the dashed lines. Cut out and glue a motif from the fabric paper to the outside of the invitation between the fold lines. Center and adhere the aged paper piece to the inside of the invitation. Cut a length of twine and insert it through the eyelet. Fold the bottom of the invitation up and then fold the top down. Wrap the twine around the invitation and tie it in a bow.

TIP Keep your invitations in character by using an Old West–style font for the letters.

RODEO SIGN

Designed by Ursula Page

Head 'em up and move 'em out for some cowpoke fun. This sign will point the way to the party. Adhere an 11½″ × 11½″ piece of wood-print fabric paper to a 12″ × 12″ piece of brown cardstock. Adhere the layered piece to a 12″ × 12″ piece of heavy cardboard. Cut out the "RODEO THIS WAY" letters from fabric paper. Adhere the letters to a darker colored card stock, leaving room around each letter. Cut around the letters ¹⁄₁₆″ from the edges so a small amount of cardstock is showing. Cut an arrow from the cardstock. Glue the letters and the arrow to the wood-print fabric paper. Add mini brads to the corners of the arrow. Embellish the sign with cowboy cutouts.

TIP Glue a length of heavy twine or small-diameter roping to the edges of the sign.

PARTY GARLAND

Hang this garland high to announce the big event. For each of the 5 letters and the 4 stars, spray the wrong side of the desired fabric paper with adhesive and place it on the wrong side of a piece of colored cardstock. Using the patterns on pages 103–109, trace the letters and stars onto the cardstock. Cut out the pieces and use a ¼″ hole punch to punch the holes where indicated on the patterns. Arrange the letters to spell "PARTY." Place a star between each letter. Lace a 2 yard length of ⅝″-wide ribbon through the holes, leaving an equal amount of ribbon extending beyond the first and last letters.

TIP Add coordinating wood beads to the ribbon as you string the letters. This will help weight down the garland if you will be hanging it outside.

Designed by Carol Kapuza

STREAMERS

You're the boss when it comes to designing these streamers. Mix and match the motifs to make each one unique or create your own letters to spell out the birthday child's name. In ours we used wooden letters purchased at a craft store. Determine the number of shapes you want on each streamer. Cut a length of jute approximately 8″ longer than the desired finished length. (For the sample streamers, we used 5 or 6 shapes spaced 2″ to 4″ apart for a 45″ streamer.) Use the patterns on page 102 and 105 to cut out 2 motifs from fabric paper for every shape you want on the streamer. For each boot and horse motif, cut 2 shapes (one in reverse). For each star motif cut out 2 shapes. The squares are 3″ × 3″.

For each streamer, form a 2″ or 3″ loop at the top with an overhand knot. Thread a 25mm wood bead onto the jute and position it under the knot. Tie a knot under the bead to keep it in place. Lay out the streamer on a long work surface. Place the desired shapes next to the streamer where they will be positioned. The first shape should be 1″ to 2″ from the bead. Apply glue to the wrong side of the first shape and place it glue side up under the jute. Lay the corresponding shape over the glued shape and press it in place. For the horse, before you glue the shape on top, cut a 1″ long piece of jute and place it on the glued shape where indicated for the tail. You may want to separate jute strands for a fuzzy tail. After the shapes are glued together, add a 7mm wiggle eye to each side where indicated and separate the 2 jute strands. The boot shapes need to be glued top to bottom where they overlap, before gluing into place.

Thread a 25mm or 16mm wood bead onto the jute and tie a knot under it. Continue to add the remaining shapes and beads, always ending with a bead or series of beads. Glue pairs of wood stars to the spaces between the shapes if desired. Cut two 12″ lengths of jute and tie them above the last shape onto the streamer.

TIP After the party, turn the streamers into a fabulous window treatment, wall hanging, or mobile for your little cowpoke's room.

Designed by Carol Kapuza

WANTED POSTER

Shoot a digital or Polaroid picture of each make-believe villain with their face in this poster as he or she arrives for the party. Before the villains get in the wagon to return to the homestead, make sure they have a copy with them. Measure and mark a line 4½″ from one short edge of a 20″ × 30″ piece of buff-colored foam core board. Use your craft knife to score the marked line, but do not cut completely through the board. Fold under the board along the scored line to create a stand-up base for the poster. Lay the board flat. Use the patterns on pages 102–109 to cut out the pieces from the desired fabric papers. Arrange the pieces on the right side of the foam core board, overlapping them slightly, and positioning the bottom of the shirt pieces above the scored edge. Refer to the photo if necessary for placement.

Designed by Susan I. Jones

TIP If you take the pictures with a camera that uses film that needs to be developed, include the processed picture with the guest's thank-you note.

With a pencil, lightly trace the opening for the cowpoke's face, using the outline of the hair and kerchief as a guide. Remove the fabric paper pieces and cut out the opening with a craft knife. Glue the fabric paper pieces to the board as they were previously arranged. Use a brown marker to outline the exposed foam core edges around the face opening. Draw a shadow around the outside of the shirt, vest, kerchief, hat, hair, letters, and stars. Indicate folds and a knot in the kerchief. With the desired color markers, make "buttons" on the shirt placket where indicated on the pattern, and add dashed lines along the placket and vest edges for topstitching.

COWPOKE PONY

These simple stick ponies hold promises of imaginary rides through the Wild West. Stitch up an entire herd for your lil' cowpoke and all his or her friends. Enlarge the pony head pattern on page 108 to the percentage indicated. Layer 2 sheets of fabric paper, wrong sides together. Using the enlarged head pattern and the ear pattern on page 102, cut out 2 heads; also cut 2 pairs of ears from the layered paper.

Cut 2 stars from a different fabric paper. Use a craft knife to make a slit on each head piece where indicated for the ears. Sew the pairs of ears wrong sides together, stitching ¼" from the curved edges and leaving the straight edge open. Pleat the bottom of each ear and insert it into an ear slit. Sew across the base of each ear. Place the heads wrong sides together.

Cut a 16" length of fringe and insert the edge of it between the head pieces where indicated on the pattern. Beginning and ending at the neck, stitch ¼" from the head edges, catching the fringe in the stitching and leaving the neck edge open.

TIP Use a bale of hay to corral the ponies when their riders are over at the chuck wagon.

Designed by Susan I. Jones

Fabric Paper Party

RoDEO

Glue a 20mm wiggle eye to each side of the head where indicated on the pattern. Cut a 3″ length of fringe in half. Glue one half above each eye to make the eyelashes.

Refer to the photo to glue jumbo rickrack or thick yarn to the pony for the bridle and reins. You will need about 3 yards. Glue a star to each side of the bridle. Stuff the pony snout with fiberfill or plastic grocery bags. Put the head on a wooden dowel or broomstick for riding.

GIFT CONTAINERS

 Happy trails can't be far away when the birthday child receives a gift in one of these special containers.

Undo a purchased lunchbox-style container by gently pulling the glued areas apart. Flatten out the box. Apply fabric glue to the outside of the box all the way to the edge. Lay the desired fabric papers over each section of the box and cut off the excess along the edges. When the glue has dried, turn the box over to the wrong side. Use a craft knife to cut the handle and side slits in the box, following the original lines. Glue the box back together along the previously glued seam. To create the tag, dip a piece of 8½˝ × 11˝ cardstock in a mixture of walnut ink and water. Let the paper dry. Create a tag on your computer and print it out on the walnut-stained cardstock. Cut the tag out and use a ¼˝ hole punch to punch a hole in the center top. Wrap a ribbon around the box, thread the ends through the tag holes, and tie the ribbon in a bow.

Cover the front and back of a plain white gift bag with fabric paper. Cut a rectangle of a different fabric paper that is 1˝ smaller than the front of the gift bag. Add a brad to each corner of the rectangle. Using your computer and printer, create a birthday greeting with Western clip art. Print it out onto cardstock. Cut the cardstock 1˝ smaller than the last rectangle of fabric paper. Apply brown ink, chalk, or metallic rub around the cardstock edges to give it an aged look. Adhere the cardstock to the bag center front. Center and adhere the completed card on the front of the gift bag. Cut a 2˝ × 12˝ strip of fabric paper. Fold the strip into thirds lengthwise, wrong sides together. Open up the strip and apply glue to the wrong side. Refold the strip and let the glue dry. Machine straight stitch through the lengthwise center of the strip. Cut the strip in half. Insert the gift into the bag. Tie the handles together with the strips.

TIP Forget the standard picnic basket; use a fabric covered box instead. Decorate one for each person and personalize the tag with his or her name.

Designed by Ursula Page

GOODY BAGS

★ Kick around one of these ideas for treat bags filled with goodies to take home, and then look out for the stampede of parents who will want your help creating bags for the next party! Add the party popper (page 92) and camera case (page 93) to the bag with the other goodies for a great surprise.

Use the patterns on pages 106 and 108 to cut 2 full boots from one fabric paper, reversing one. From a contrasting fabric paper, cut 1 each of the boot top, trim, and toe; cut 2 stars. Refer to the photo to position the top, trim, and toe pieces on one of the full boot pieces, placing the trim ends under the top and toe pieces. Position the stars on each side of the trim. Use a small amount of glue to temporarily hold the pieces in place. Stitch ¼″ from the top and bottom curved edges of the top piece. Edgestitch the trim piece along both long edges. On the toe, stitch ¼″ from the curved upper edge only. Place the appliquéd boot and the remaining boot piece wrong sides together. Stitch ¼″ from the outer edges, leaving the top curved edge open.

★ Cover the front and back of a plain white craft bag with fabric paper. Cover the sides with a different fabric paper. Align the top edges of the bag. Trim along the edges with decorative-edge scissors. Fold the top of the bag over approximately 1½″. Use a ¼″ hole punch to punch 2 holes in the folded over flap through all of the bag layers, approximately 1″ from the sides. Thread a length of ribbon through the holes and tie the ends together on the front of the flap. Thread a charm onto one ribbon end and then tie the ends together again to knot.

TIP Fill the bags with shredded brown paper or natural raffia strips before adding the candy to give them a fuller look.

Designed by Susan I. Jones

Designed by Ursula Page

Party Popper

Designed by Susan I. Jones

This party favor is a snap to make and guarantees the cowpokes a bang-up time. Center and tape the snap device inside an empty toilet paper tube. Cover one end of the tube with a square of aluminum foil, allowing the snapper end to stick out. Fill the tube with the selected favors. Cap the open end with another square of foil in the same manner as before, allowing the popper end to stick out.

Pink the short sides of a 5½″ × 12″ rectangle of fabric paper. Lay the rectangle wrong side up. Position the filled tube in the center of the rectangle and glue one long edge of the fabric paper to the tube. Roll the tube in the fabric paper and secure the edge with glue. Cut a 3″ square from another fabric paper, placing the motif on point. Pink the edges of the square. Center and glue the square to the tube's glued edge. Tie raffia around the excess fabric paper at the ends of the tube. To create the noise, grab both ends of the snap device and pull sharply. Untie the raffia to reveal the goodies.

TIP Consider filling the tubes with non candy items such as crayons, small plastic animals, or bubble-blowing liquid. Check out your local party supply store for lots of other kid-friendly trinkets.

CAMERA CASE

Kids love to take pictures. They'll be all smiles when you hand these out at the end of the party or include them in their goody bags. Purchase your cameras first. Measure the camera and make a pattern for the case. Cut out 1 case from paper to check the size. Adjust the pattern as needed to accommodate the camera. Adhere 2 pieces of fabric paper wrong sides together. Use the pattern to cut out 1 case from the layered fabric paper. Fold the box where indicated on the pattern. Glue the tabs to the bottom and front. Cut out a motif from another fabric paper and glue it to the box lid. Place the camera inside the box and tie it shut with string or jute.

TIP If your cowpokes are too young for cameras, make the boxes and fill them with a couple of cookies or an individually packaged snack cake.

Designed by Carol Kapuza

THANK-YOU CARD

Good little cowpokes will be sure to send these special notes to all their friends, thanking them for their gifts and a fun time. Cut a piece of poster board the width of the finished note and twice the length. Place a ruler on the center of the paper and lightly score the paper along the edge to be folded. Fold the paper in half, wrong sides together. Cover all but the back of the folded piece with separate pieces of fabric paper. Cut out a coordinating square of fabric paper for the card front. Wrap a length of ribbon around the bottom of the square, crossing the ends at the center front. Use your craft knife to cut a small slit in the ribbons where they cross. Insert a brad through the hole and fabric paper. Glue the piece to the front of the card, aligning the lower edges and leaving some of the background fabric exposed on the top and sides.

Using your computer and printer, print out the inside message and "Thank You" on cardstock. Cut out each piece, leaving some blank space around the edges. Rub brown ink or chalk around the edges of each piece to give it an aged look. Glue the "Thank You" piece to the top front of the card **and have your cowpoke sign his or her name**. Cut out a cowboy motif from fabric paper and glue it under the "Thank You" piece. Use a ⅛" hole punch to punch holes in the 4 corners of the message piece. Set an eyelet in each hole. Thread a length of ribbon through the eyelets on each side and tie the ribbon ends in a knot on the front. Glue the message to the inside of the card.

TIP Make sure someone makes a list of what gifts your child received and from whom so you can personalize the messages.

Dear Joshua,

Thank you so much for coming to my birthday party. We had a rootin'-tootin' time! I love the vest and spurs you gave me. I am glad we are friends.

Sterling

Designed by Ursula Page

Photo Frames

Designed by Ursula Page

Long after the gang has ridden off into the sunset, these covered picture frames will remind you of all the fun. Purchase a frame with a smooth, flat surface. Remove the glass and backing and set them aside. Apply fabric decoupage medium to the front of the frame. Place the fabric paper over the decoupage medium, making sure there is a large enough border of fabric paper to cover the edges. Use a craft knife to carefully cut diagonally from corner to corner through the picture opening. Fold the fabric paper in the opening to the wrong side to cover the opening edges; glue the excess in place on the back of the opening. Wrap the sides of the frame; cut off any excess fabric paper flush with the edge. Decorate the frame with cowboy cutouts, ribbons, and paper or metal nameplates.

TIP Coat the frame with fabric decoupage medium to make it more durable and look leather-like. Add ribbons and raised nameplates after the glue has dried.

SCRAPBOOK PAGE

The memory of those sweet little wannabe cowboys will always be near when you fix yerself up with a batch of scrapbook pages that feature pictures from the party.

While in Arizona on a business trip, I was given cowboy hats and bandanas as souvenirs. I brought them home for the boys and Preston immediately fell in love with his hat, even though it was way too big on him! He spent the next few days wearing the hat everywhere around the house and he looked so cute!

Designed by Ursula Page

PATTERNS

Asian Dinner
Party
Circle Butterfly
Streamers

Medium

Asian Dinner
Party
Circle butterfly
Streamer

Small

Asian Dinner
Party

Large
Circle Butterfly
Streamer

Asian Dinner Party
Water Lily

chocolate holder
sake carafe

Asian Dinner Party

Chopstick Holder
Basic Butterlfy Streamers
Paper Lanterns

Place on Fold

Asian Dinner
Party

Basic
Small
Butterfly

Harvest Wedding

Wish Tag

Harvest Wedding

Wish Tag

Place on Fold

Hole placement for
chop stick holder

Place on Fold

Asian Dinner Party
Basic
Medium
Butterfly

Asian Dinner Party

Water Lily
Chocolate Holder
Base

Harvest Wedding

Rose
Calyx

Harvest Wedding

Sunflower
Calyx

Harvest Wedding

Poppy
Calyx

Harvest Wedding

Iris
Petal

Harvest Wedding

Poppy
Petal

Pleat

Harvest
Wedding
Daisy
Petal

Pleat

Harvest
Wedding
Camera
Bag Tag

Pleat

Harvest Wedding Sunflower Petal

Harvest
Wedding
Small
Rose Petal

Harvest Wedding
Large
Rose Petal

Harvest Wedding
Wish Tag
and
Asian Dinner
Party Tags

Harvest Wedding
Wish Tag
and
Asian Dinner
Party Tags

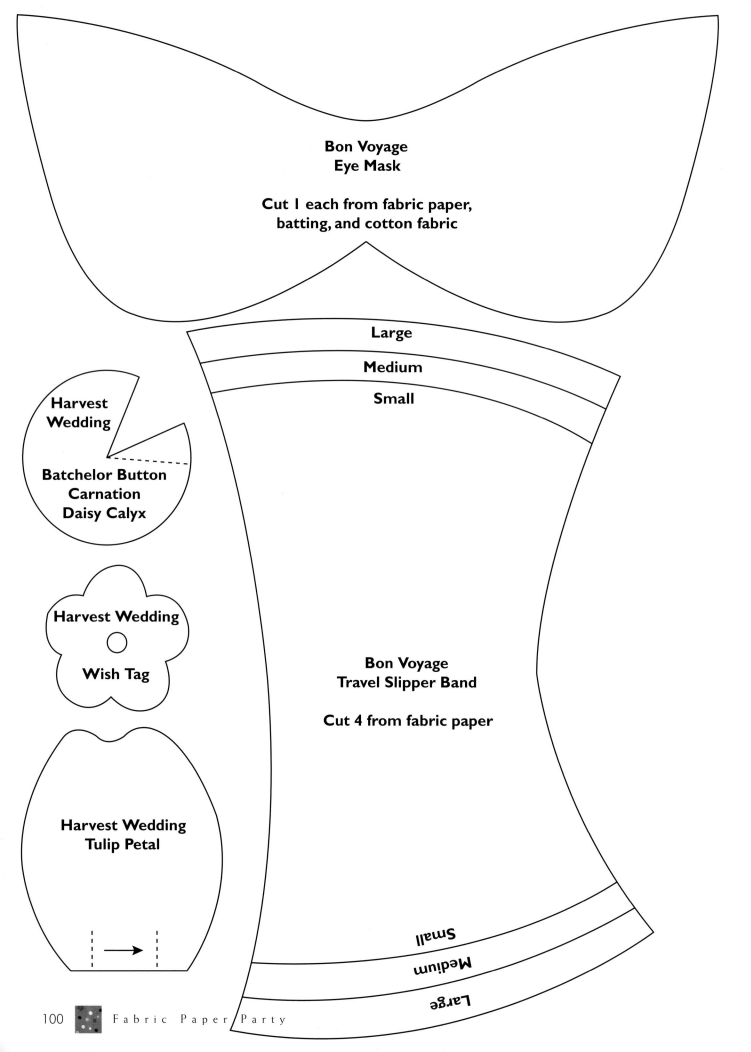

**Bon Voyage
Eye Mask**

**Cut 1 each from fabric paper,
batting, and cotton fabric**

Large

Medium

Small

**Harvest
Wedding**

**Batchelor Button
Carnation
Daisy Calyx**

Harvest Wedding

Wish Tag

**Bon Voyage
Travel Slipper Band**

Cut 4 from fabric paper

**Harvest Wedding
Tulip Petal**

Small

Medium

Large

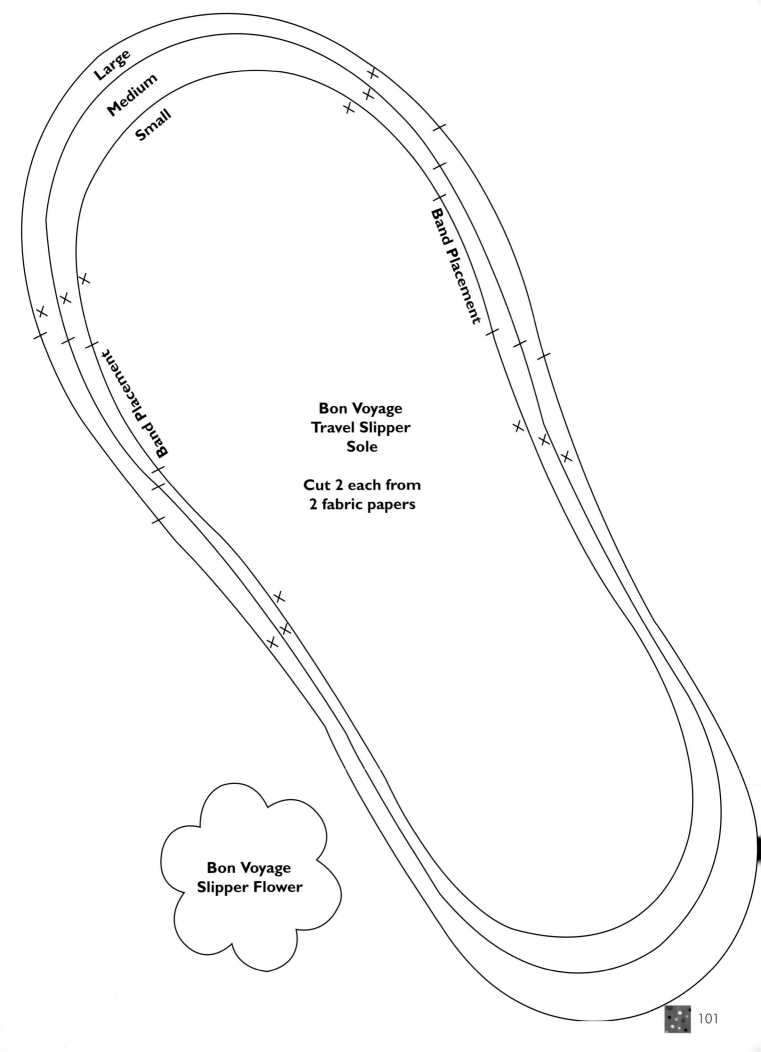

Large

Medium

Small

Band Placement

Band Placement

Bon Voyage
Travel Slipper
Sole

Cut 2 each from
2 fabric papers

Bon Voyage
Slipper Flower

101

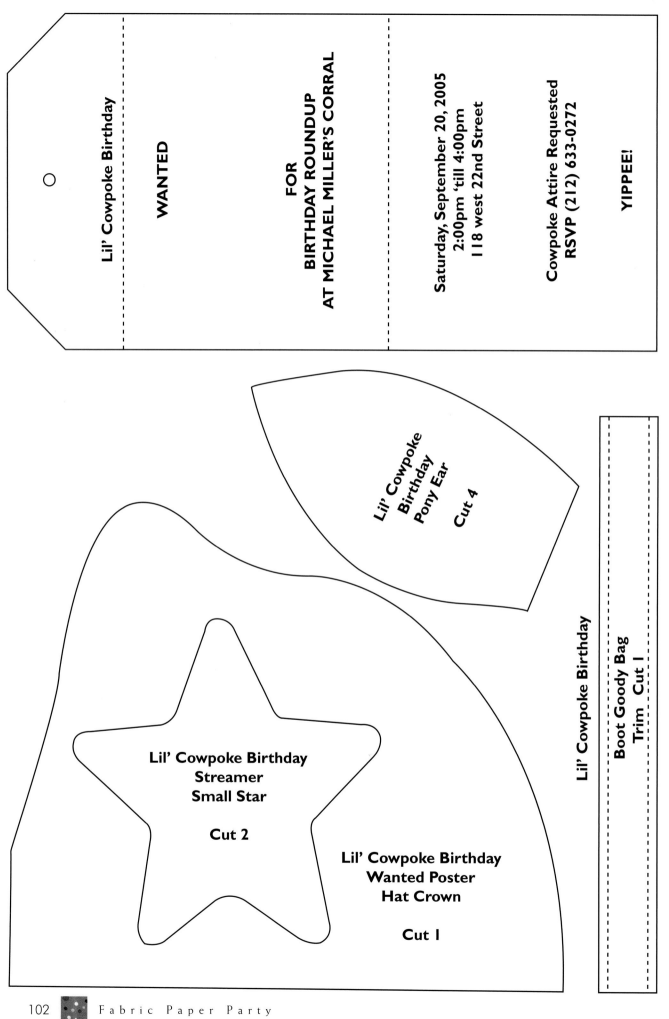

Lil' Cowpoke Birthday

WANTED

FOR
BIRTHDAY ROUNDUP
AT MICHAEL MILLER'S CORRAL

Saturday, September 20, 2005
2:00pm 'till 4:00pm
118 west 22nd Street

Cowpoke Attire Requested
RSVP (212) 633-0272

YIPPEE!

Lil' Cowpoke
Birthday
Pony Ear

Cut 4

Lil' Cowpoke Birthday

Boot Goody Bag
Trim Cut 1

Lil' Cowpoke Birthday
Streamer
Small Star

Cut 2

Lil' Cowpoke Birthday
Wanted Poster
Hat Crown

Cut 1

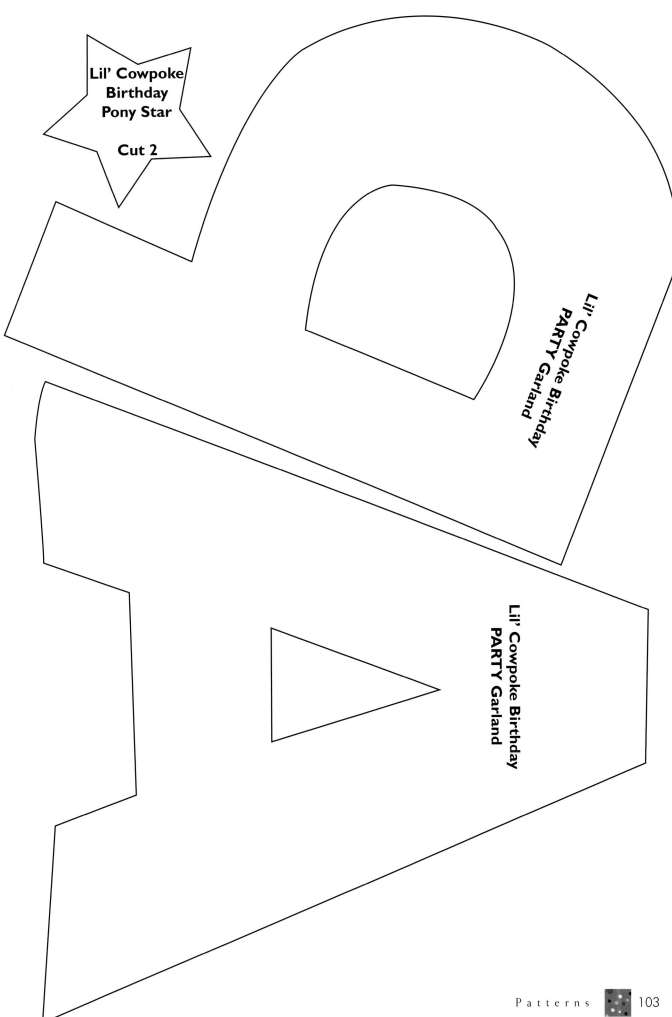

Lil' Cowpoke
Birthday
Pony Star

Cut 2

Lil' Cowpoke Birthday
PARTY Garland

Lil' Cowpoke Birthday
PARTY Garland

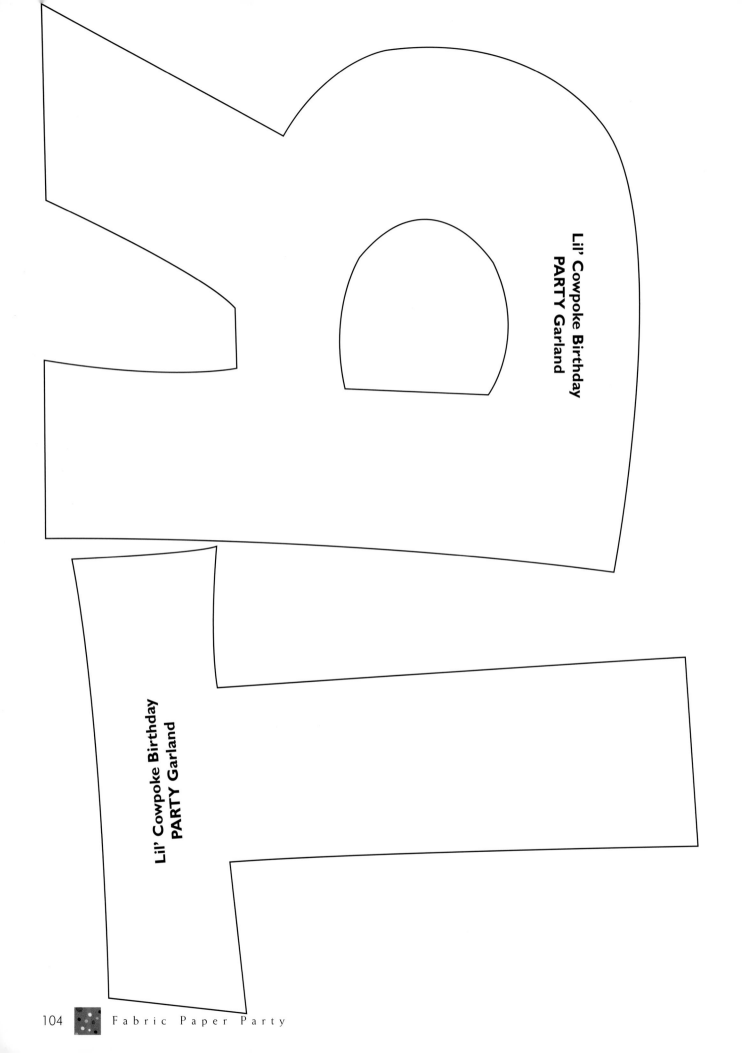

Lil' Cowpoke Birthday
PARTY Garland

Lil' Cowpoke Birthday
PARTY Garland

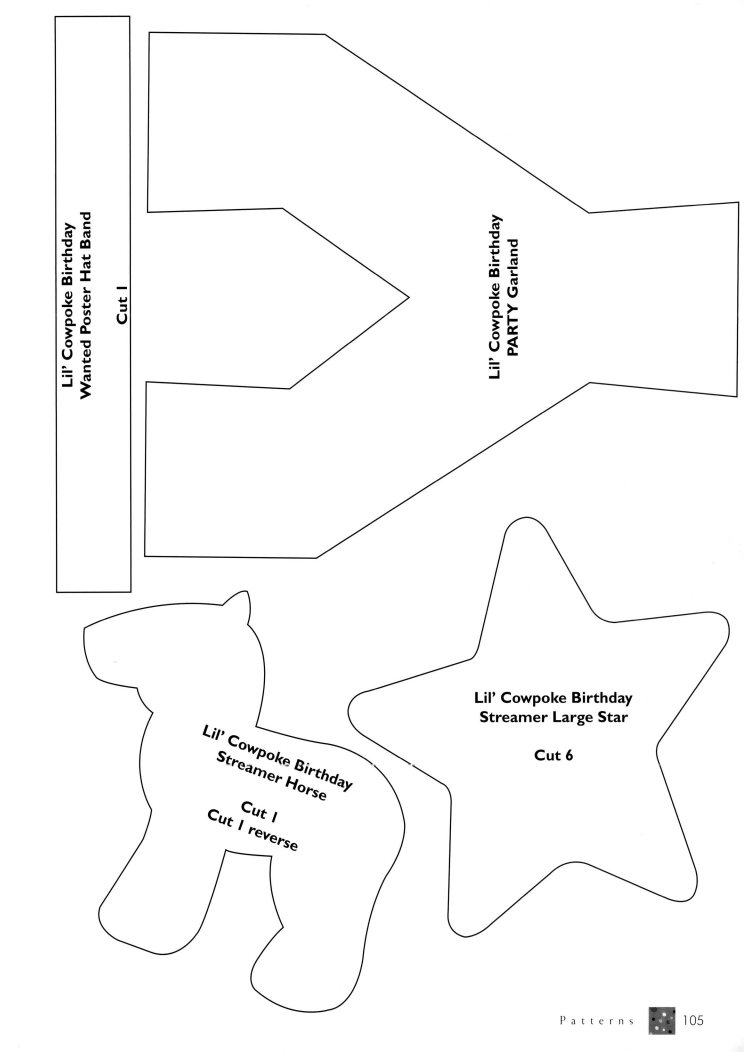

**Lil' Cowpoke Birthday
Wanted Poster Hat Band**

Cut 1

**Lil' Cowpoke Birthday
PARTY Garland**

**Lil' Cowpoke Birthday
Streamer Large Star**

Cut 6

**Lil' Cowpoke Birthday
Streamer Horse**

**Cut 1
Cut 1 reverse**

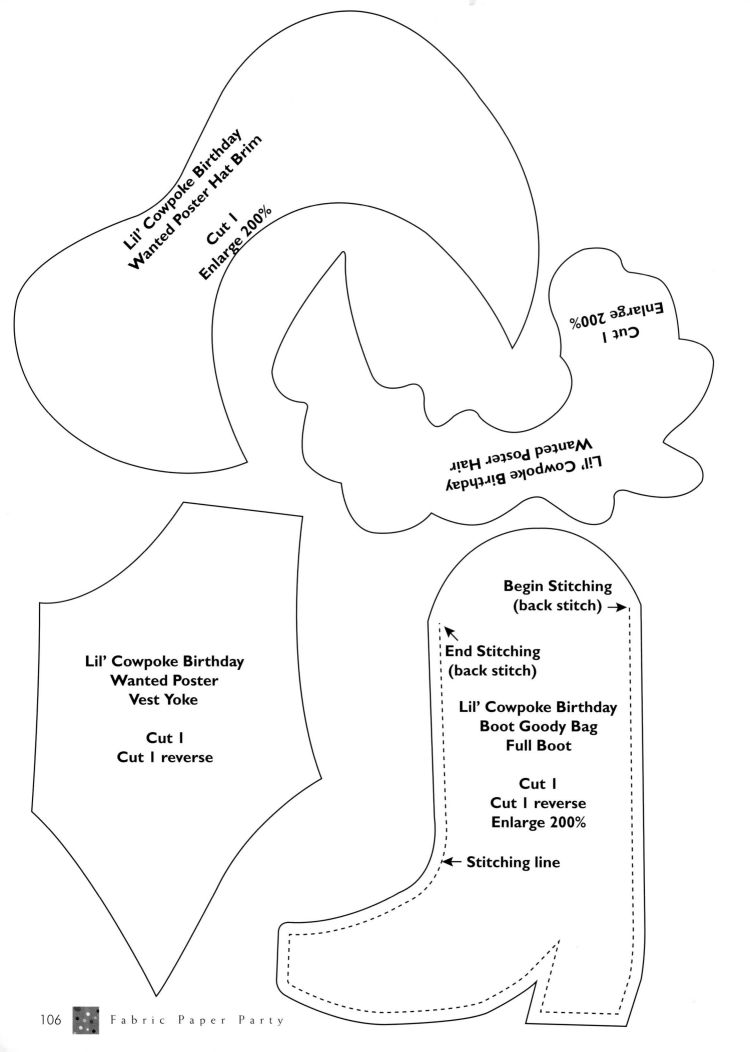

Lil' Cowpoke Birthday
Wanted Poster Hat Brim

Cut I
Enlarge 200%

Enlarge 200%

Cut I

Lil' Cowpoke Birthday
Wanted Poster Hair

Lil' Cowpoke Birthday
Wanted Poster
Vest Yoke

Cut I
Cut I reverse

Begin Stitching
(back stitch) →

End Stitching
(back stitch)

Lil' Cowpoke Birthday
Boot Goody Bag
Full Boot

Cut I
Cut I reverse
Enlarge 200%

← Stitching line

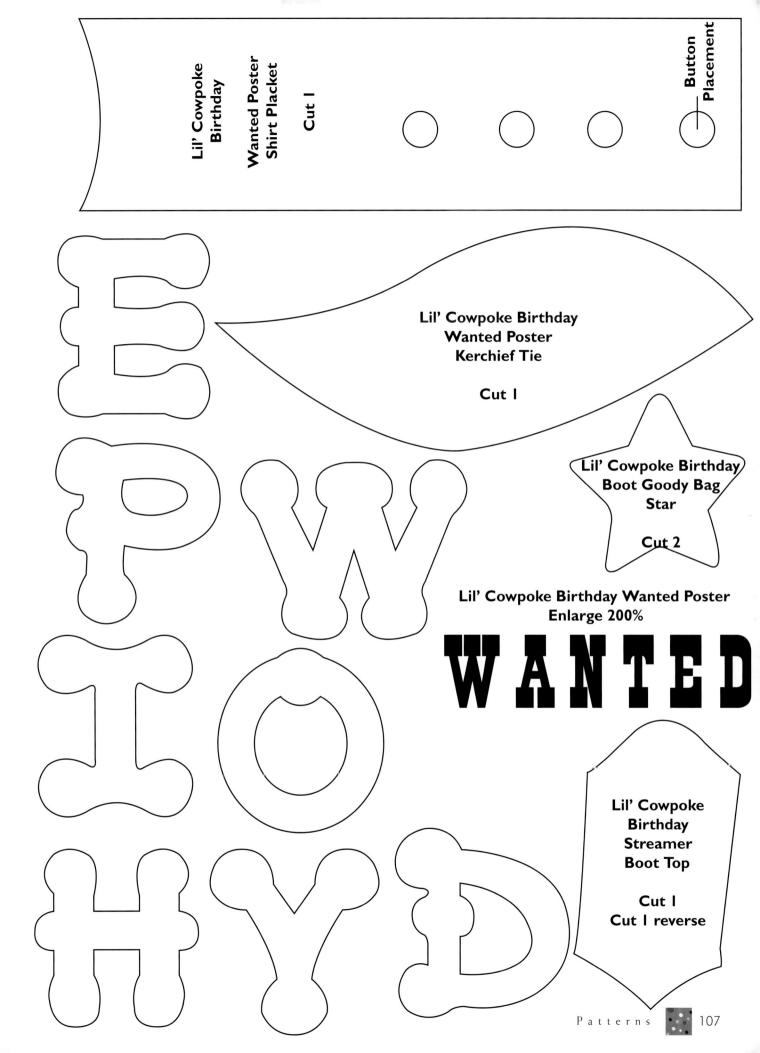

Lil' Cowpoke Birthday
Wanted Poster
Shirt Placket

Cut 1

Button
Placement

Lil' Cowpoke Birthday
Wanted Poster
Kerchief Tie

Cut 1

Lil' Cowpoke Birthday
Boot Goody Bag
Star

Cut 2

Lil' Cowpoke Birthday Wanted Poster
Enlarge 200%

WANTED

Lil' Cowpoke
Birthday
Streamer
Boot Top

Cut 1
Cut 1 reverse

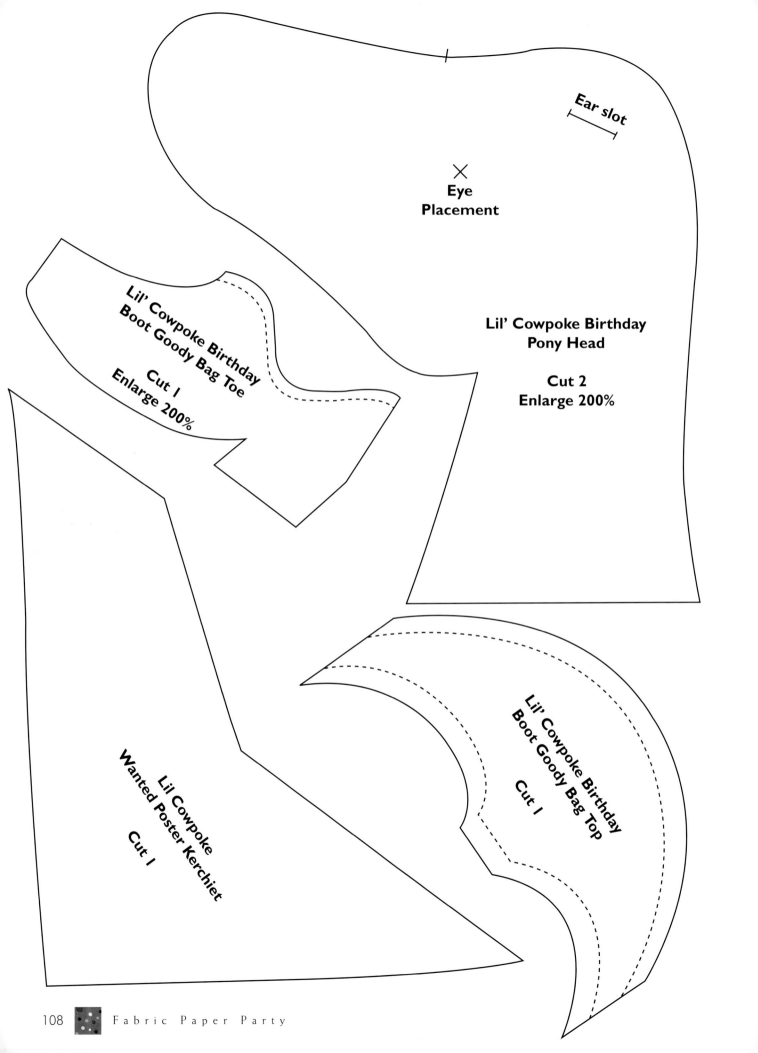

Ear slot

✕
**Eye
Placement**

**Lil' Cowpoke Birthday
Boot Goody Bag Toe**

**Cut 1
Enlarge 200%**

**Lil' Cowpoke Birthday
Pony Head**

**Cut 2
Enlarge 200%**

**Lil' Cowpoke Birthday
Boot Goody Bag Top**

Cut 1

**Lil Cowpoke
Wanted Poster Kerchief**

Cut 1

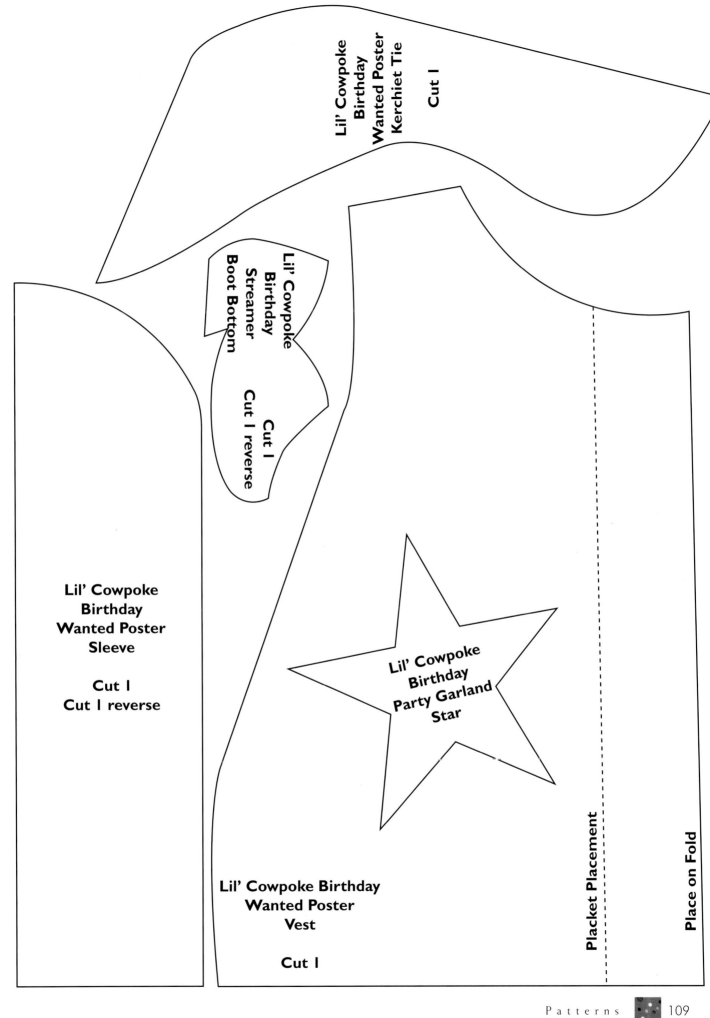

Lil' Cowpoke
Birthday
Wanted Poster
Kerchiet Tie

Cut 1

Lil' Cowpoke
Birthday
Streamer
Boot Bottom

Cut 1
Cut 1 reverse

Lil' Cowpoke
Birthday
Wanted Poster
Sleeve

Cut 1
Cut 1 reverse

Lil' Cowpoke
Birthday
Party Garland
Star

Lil' Cowpoke Birthday
Wanted Poster
Vest

Cut 1

Placket Placement

Place on Fold

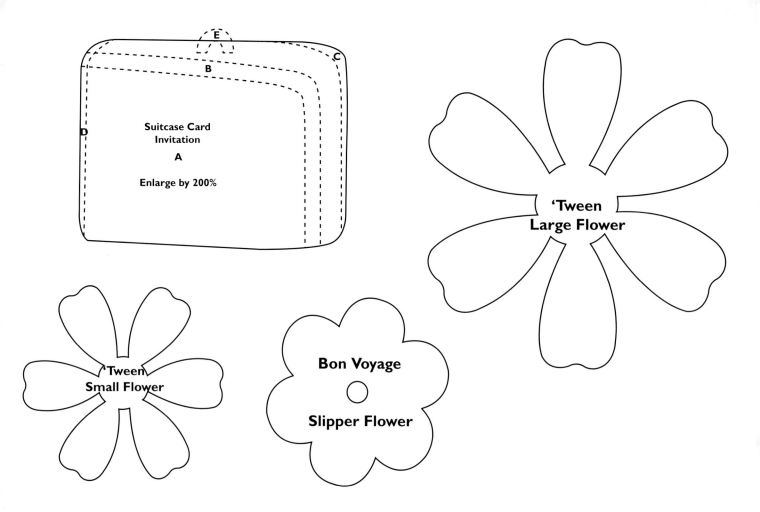

Suitcase Card
Invitation
A

Enlarge by 200%

'Tween
Large Flower

'Tween
Small Flower

Bon Voyage

Slipper Flower

SOURCES

**All supplies listed are available at scrapbook and craft stores unless otherwise noted. For a complete selection of the fabric papers used in these projects as well as other possibilities and the location of a store near you, visit: michaelmillermemories.com

Asian Dinner Party:
Butterfly Chopstick Holder:
Fabric paper
¼" hole punch
Chalk and applicator:
Ultra fine glitter
Clear drying adhesive with a fine tip applicator: "Barbara Trombley's Art glittering system"
Pop dots: self adhesive foam mounts
Beacon "Hold the foam" adhesive

Butterfly Streamers:
Fabric paper
Novelty yarns: fiberGoddess@msn.com
Glitter glue
Sparkle Mod Podge
Asian coins or metal washers to tie on end of yarn as weights

Scissors or die cuts for shapes
Beacon "Hold the foam" adhesiv

Water Lilly chocolate holder:
Fabric paper
Heat gun
Chalk and applicator
Pop dots: self adhesive foam mounts
Sponge brush applicator
Glitter glue or Sparkle Mod Podge
Bamboo skewer: (optional) for use with heat gun to keep fingers away from heat
Chocolate of choice: Ferre Roche

Tags:
Fabric paper
Pop dots: self adhesive foam mounts
Gold acrylic paint
Glitter glue
Assorted ribbons and cords

Luminaries:
Fabric paper
Aluminum vent cover (2" wider than circumference of candle) available at your local hardware store
Spray paint:black matte
Beacon "hold the foam" adhesive

Cowboy Party:
Thank You Card:
Ribbon: Michael's and unknown
Eyelets: Making Memories
Brad: Big Lots (generic brand)
Cardstock: Bazzill
Ink: Nick Bantock by Ranger Industries
Font: Edmunds

Sterling & Henry Frame
Frame
Mod Podge
Cardstock: Bazzill
Ink: Nick Bantock by Ranger Industries
Stamps: PSX

Preston Frame
Frame
Ribbon: Unknown
Paper "Buttons": K&Co
Frame: K&Co
Cardstock: Bazzill
Ink: Nick Bantock by Ranger Industries
Stamps: PSX

Scrapbook Page
Cardstock: Bazzill
Ink: Nick Bantock by Ranger Industries

Giddyup sign and frame: K&Co
Acrylic frame: Paperbilities
Letter Stickers: Sonnets by Sharon Soneff
for Creative Imaginations
Conchos: Scrapworks
Ribbon:
Fonts: Rope MF and CK Corral (by
Creating Keepsakes)
Brads: Making Memories

Box Gift Container
Cardstock: Bazzill
Ink: Nick Bantock by Ranger Industries
Ribbon:
Font: Edmunds
Box:
Clip Art: Microsoft
Hole Punch: Fiskars

Gift Bag
Cardstock: Bazzill
Ink: Nick Bantock by Ranger Industries
Fonts: Rope MF and CK Corral (by
Creating Keepsakes)
Bag:
Clip Art: Microsoft
Chalk: Chalklets by EK Success
Brads

Invitation:
Cardstock: Bazzill
Twine/hemp cord: Stampin' Up
Font: Edmunds
Poster board:
Mod Podge
Ink: Nick Bantock by Ranger Industries

Goody Bag:
Ribbon:
Charm: Card Connection
White bag:

Sign:
Cardstock: Bazzill
Brads: Making Memories
Font: AppleScruffs

Cowboy Party/Tween:

Party Popper:
Popper snap components are available
from Olde English Crackers, 106 Briza
Court, Bellingham, WA 98229; phone
(877) 606-2972 or visit the Website at
www.oldenglishcrackers.com.

Asian Dinner Party:

Take Out Box:
Ribbon:
Brad:
Take Out Box

Magnets:
High-Energy Dyna-mite magnetic but-
tons
Glass Pebbles:
Tin:

Candles:
Ribbon:
Lock Charm: Collage Secrets
Glitter: Mark Enterprises

Place card:
Chipboard
Vellum: Paper Adventures
Font: SF Shai Fontai
Embossing Powder: Stamp-N-Stuff by
Mark Enterprises
Ink: Versamark by Tsukineko
Ribbon

Invitation:
Chipboard
Vellum: Paper Adventures
Font: SF Shai Fontai
Embossing Powder: Stamp-N-Stuff by
Mark Enterprises
Ink: Versamark by Tsukineko
Ribbon:
Bead: Blue Moon Beads
Elastic

Menu Card:
Chipboard
Vellum: Paper Adventures
Font: SF Shai Fontai
Embossing Powder: Stamp-N-Stuff by
Mark Enterprises
Ink: Versamark by Tsukineko
Ribbon
Bamboo Holders: 7 Gypsies
Bow Charm:

Bon Voyage Party:

Memories Box:
Paper Mache Box
Ribbon: May Arts
Book Plate: www.twopeasinabucket.com
Cardstock: Bazzill
Font: Girls Are Weird
Brads: ScrapEssentials by JoAnn's

Friends Album:
Ribbon:
Slide Mount: www.scrapsahoy.com
Cardstock: Bazzill
Sticker: Bo-Bunny Press

Wedding:
Guest Book:
Ribbon:
Heart Paper Clips: Cardmaker's Accents
Metal Letters: ScrapEssentials by JoAnn's
Acrylic Paint: Plaid

Favor Boxes
Rub-Ons: Making Memories
Letter Stickers: Wordsworth
Conchos: Darice
Ribbon
Heart Paper Clips: Cardmaker's Accents
Metal Tag: Making Memories
Mod Podge
Letter Stickers: Sonnets by Sharon
Sonneff for Creative Imaginations
Slide Mount: www.scrapsahoy.com
Silk Ribbon:
Metal Heart: Making Memories
Metal Letters: Making Memories

Match Boxes:
Love Sticker:
Ribbon:
Heart Paper Clip: Cardmaker's Accents
Heart Sticker: Jolee's Boutique by EK
Success

CD Box:
Letter Stickers: Wordsworth
Ribbon:
Metal Tag: Making Memories
Brad: The Happy Hammer
Door Knocker: 7 Gypsies
Box: AOL free trial box

Invitation:
Twine/Hemp Cord: Stampin' Up
Vellum: Paper Adventures
Font: Allegro
Embossing Powder: Stamp-N-Stuff by
Mark Enterprises and Clearsnap
Ink: Versamark by Tsukineko
Ribbon:
Brads: Making Memories
Metal "&": Making Memories

ABOUT THE AUTHOR AND CONTRIBUTING ARTISTS

Kathy Miller Sonoma, California

Who knew that traveling; sewing her own clothes; and batik, painting, and screen printing classes were all life experiences that would lead Kathy to New York City and a 30-year career in the textile industry? Designing fabrics for large and small corporations within the women's sportswear, eveningwear, lingerie, and home-sewing trade formed the foundation for her success as co-president of Michael Miller Fabrics LLC. The company caters to the whims and wishes of the quilting and fashion world and has received many awards for its unique designs and marketing.

Ursula Page Thomasville, Georgia

Ursula Page recently left the world of healthcare to become a full-time mother to her two boys, Sterling and Preston. The change has allowed her to spend more time as a craft and scrapbook designer, as well as remodel the old house she and her husband, Chris, recently purchased. Ursula has loved crafts from an early age and in 1997 began scrapbooking. Her style has evolved greatly over the years and has become truly unique and identifiable. Not only does she have an innate talent for combining colors and patterns to express many different moods in her layout, she is also able to choose embellishments and techniques that complement her photos and journaling perfectly. Ursula's work has been featured in *Creating Keepsakes, Scrapbooks, etc., Memory Makers, PaperKuts,* and *Scrapbook Trends.*

Susan I. Jones Chandler, Arizona

Specializing in one-of-a-kind fiber art for more than 25 years, Susan has designed and produced costumes for the theater and dance, as well as textile art for advertising and set design. Susan's fiber art has been published in six books and many fiber-related magazines. She has designed wearable art for invitational international fashion shows and exhibits. Several fabric companies and related manufacturers feature her work to promote new product lines. Susan is currently pursuing her own mixed-media fiber art.

Marinda Stewart Santa Maria, California

Designer, author, and teacher Marinda Stewart started her creative endeavors at an early age. In addition to being the author of five books, her accomplishments include a line of patterns, countless magazine and book contributions, television appearances, national ads, and museum and gallery exhibitions. Her work is in the collections of several corporations and celebrities. Currently, she works with corporate clients designing and consulting on end uses for their products.

Carol Kapuza Los Angeles, California

Carol is a noted textile artist whose innovative designs have received critical acclaim in theatrical, fashion, and educational circles. Over the past two decades, she has created a striking career tapestry with intertwined strands as diverse as Shakespearean costumes, sweater and jean embroidery for major clothing design companies, massive outdoor art, and studio instruction. Carol extends a heartfelt thank-you to Kathy Miller for introducing her to scrapbooking and fabric paper.

Marah Johnson Oceanside, California

Experimentation is the key to Marah's art. Growing up with an artist mother and a storyteller and author father, she has never been one to be driven by the norm. Marah is always striving to try something new, whether it is a combination of colors, textures, or techniques. It is this fearless willingness to try the unknown that has led her to her success as an artist. On any given day of the week you can find Marah in her studio with a blowtorch in one hand and a paintbrush in the other. She resides in Oceanside with her husband and three daughters.